$1.00
6/8
EH

UCEA Leadership Series

1. Joseph Murphy. *Preparing School Leaders: Defining a Research and Action Agenda*. 2006.
2. Fenwick W. English and Gail C. Furman. *Research and Educational Leadership: Navigating the New National Research Council Guidelines*. 2007.

Research and Educational Leadership

Navigating the New National Research Council Guidelines

Edited by
Fenwick W. English
Gail C. Furman

Published in partnership with the
University Council for Educational Administration

Rowman & Littlefield Education
Lanham, Maryland • Toronto • Plymouth, UK
2007

Published in partnership with the
University Council for Educational Administration

Published in the United States of America
by Rowman & Littlefield Education
A Division of Rowman & Littlefield Publishers, Inc.
A wholly owned subsidary of The Rowman & Littlefield Publishing Group, Inc.
4501 Forbes Boulevard, Suite 200, Lanham, Maryland 20706
www.rowmaneducation.com

Estover Road
Plymouth PL6 7PY
United Kingdom

British Library Cataloguing in Publication Information Available

Library of Congress Cataloging-in-Publication Data

Research and educational leadership : navigating the new National Research
Council guidelines / edited by Fenwick W. English, Gail C. Furman.
      p. cm. — (UCEA leadership series)
   "Published in partnership with the University Council for Educational
Administration."
   Includes bibliographical references and index.
   ISBN-13: 978-1-57886-550-5 (hardcover : alk. paper)
   ISBN-13: 978-1-57886-551-2 (pbk. : alk. paper)
   ISBN-10: 1-57886-550-6 (hardcover : alk. paper)
   ISBN-10: 1-57886-551-4 (pbk. : alk. paper)
   1. Education—Research. 2. Educational leadership. 3. Educational leadership—
Research. 4. National Research Council (U.S.) I. English, Fenwick W. II. Furman,
Gail C. III. University Council for Educational Administration.
   LB1028.2.R47 2007
   370.7'2—dc22   2006026144

Contents

Foreword

Gary M. Crow, The Florida State University

Over 50 years ago, the University Council for Educational Administration (UCEA) began its work to improve the professional preparation of educational leaders. A major component of its work then and now was to "continue efforts toward standards of excellence in research." Obviously, this early work of UCEA reflected the perspectives on scientific research prevalent in the 1950s, as evidenced by one of the original purposes of "shifting educational administration from an anecdotal orientation to a more scientific one, leading to generalizations about organizations and leadership." In the complex and dynamic environment of debate around the nature of educational research today, this purpose is far from uncontested. UCEA's current purpose, however, continues to emphasize the importance and rigor of research to ensure effectiveness, equity and social justice for all students, families, and educators.

This book follows the track of this early purpose of UCEA and seeks to explore the implications of a significant national event in the process of defining and improving research for educational leadership. This event— the publication of *Scientific Research in Education* by the National Research Council (NRC)—offers an important opportunity for diverse scholars in the field of educational leadership to address the philosophical, political, historical, cultural, and practical implications of scientific research for educational leadership. The authors of this book provide an excellent response to the implications of the NRC document.

As graduate students, professors, and policymakers, we struggle with at least two major issues of research to improve leadership and the schools we serve: relevance and rigor. This book, by responding to the assertions made in the NRC publication, provides a series of excellent observations and critiques of the assertions and, more importantly, provides an opportunity to enliven the discourse around the relevance and rigor of research in our field.

Gall, Gall, and Borg (2003), authors of a popular text on educational research, comment that if medical doctors lost their base of medical knowledge they would have to cease their practice. However, if educators suddenly lost their base of knowledge gained through research, nothing would change. The relevance of research for theory, practice, and policy is an ongoing struggle for each new generation of educational researchers. Although the very nature of relevance is replete with philosophical, political, and conceptual dilemmas, attempts to "make a difference" with our research are important for effectiveness, equity, and social justice as they impact student learning, school change, leadership actions, and the preparation and professional development of school and district leaders. Educational researchers lament the disregard by policymakers of research to inform major policy decisions as well as school leadership practice. Laying blame for this problem is seldom useful for changing it. The book by English, Furman, and their colleagues, however, provides useful perspectives in understanding broader and deeper contexts for relevance and motivates us to keep relevance central to our research purposes.

In addition to relevance, educational research for leadership must be concerned with rigor. Again, this is not an uncontested term, as the various perspectives in the book clearly illustrate. There are, without question, philosophical, political, cultural and historical differences surrounding rigor and how to achieve it. These differences are important and the authors provide excellent arguments for how they affect the nature of what is researched, how it is researched and why it is researched. But the contested nature of rigor does not give us an excuse for ignoring or eliminating it from our concern and action as researchers. It seems clear after reading this book that at least two issues of rigor need our attention. First, standards of research are not the same as standardization of research practice. As researchers, we can and should develop, implement, and continually assess our standards for educational research that contribute to making a difference for all students, their families, and educators. Acknowledging and using standards for rigor in educational research does not mean standardizing the practice of research so that only certain types of research are valued, funded, or deemed relevant for educational leadership.

Second, these authors remind us of the necessity and value of an ongoing dialogue about rigor. Viewing the history of research provides ample evidence of this ongoing struggle to define different ways to maintain rigor in research. Emerging research methodologies, paradigms and purposes are the latest instances in that history. Educational research, like any intellectual endeavor, has a developmental nature in which research paradigms, methods, and views of rigor evolve. However, as Shields point out in her chapter, this does not necessitate a relativistic position in which anything or nothing goes in terms of rigor.

Standards of rigor are indeed value-laden but that is not a weakness. The response to the need for rigor in educational research, however, as these chapters show, should not be a government-imposed, or even profession-imposed, narrow set of definitions. Rather, as this book superbly argues, the discussion of research rigor must acknowledge multiple perspectives, multiple purposes, and multiple views of rigor.

The book contributes to what can be an exciting and valuable dialogue regarding research rigor in educational leadership research. This does not mean, as Shields reminds us, that the purpose of this dialogue is to reach consensus. Rather, the purpose of this dialogue is to enrich the understanding and practice of rigor in our multiple research purposes, paradigms and methods.

During the last several years, I believe we have weakened both the practice and the assumed value of such discourse. We have built fences around our research and views of rigor that do not allow dialogue, but rather silence differences. Such isolation benefits neither the relevance nor the rigor of our research. This book is a valuable tool to use in regaining and reinvigorating this dialogue, because the authors raise the kinds of pertinent issues about relevance and rigor that deserve the attention of all researchers in educational leadership. In addition to its value for researchers, this book can be a useful tool in educational leadership courses to expose graduate students to the debates around the relevance and rigor of educational research and to enhance their own research.

I commend each of the authors in this book for stimulating the dialogue in our profession on the relevance and rigor of educational research. They all have contributed to that continuing purpose of UCEA to inform and improve research that benefits all students, families, and educators.

Introduction

*Fenwick W. English, University of North Carolina at Chapel Hill;
and Gail C. Furman, Washington State University*

This is a book about research in educational leadership and school administration. It was sparked by the 2002 release of the publication *Scientific Research in Education* by the National Research Council (NRC) co-edited by Richard Shavelson and Lisa Towne.

No work, even an allegedly scientific one, is value neutral. *Scientific Research in Education* is not an exception. As this book will make clear, *Scientific Research in Education* has to be viewed as one of many kinds of national reports recently released which have been critical of educational leadership, educational research and education in general. We therefore view the NRC's efforts with a mixture of some agreement with the concept of enhanced research rigor along with skepticism, particularly with regard to its impact in and on education.

Scientific Research in Education provoked unusual interest about research in education in general, and research methods in education specifically, leading to lively and sometimes heated debate in the national education research community. Such dialogue occurred largely, though not exclusively, at American Education Research Association (AERA) and for professors of educational leadership, at University Council for Educational Administration (UCEA).

Shortly after the release of *Scientific Research in Education*, the UCEA Executive Committee discussed the advisability of publishing some scholarly papers, which had been blind reviewed and later presented at AERA's and UCEA's annual conferences, that were centered on some of the premises and postulates of *Scientific Research in Education*. This book represents a distillation of some of the broad band of responses to them during the subsequent two-year time period that followed and preceded this book.

While *Scientific Research in Education* was not aimed specifically at research in or about educational leadership or school administration, it nonetheless has important and far-reaching implications for its conduct in our field. It is of particular importance for the doctoral granting institutions that comprise the exclusive membership of more than seventy-five programs belonging to UCEA. For all institutions whose faculty and/or students are engaged in educational research, this book can point out what types of research offer an expanded promise to reground the discipline in the future.

The purposes of this book are to:

1. Undertake a critical examination of the major premises advanced in *Scientific Research in Education*, and explore the implications of these premises for research on educational leadership and school administration. This examination will include areas where the science proffered in the NRC's work will or will not be helpful in constructing a better understanding of the phenomenon of leadership in educational settings;
2. Open the discourse about research in educational leadership to include a wider perspective than that outlined in *Scientific Research in Education*;
3. Identify how *Scientific Research in Education* might advance knowledge of the field and open up new vistas of understanding, where future research is needed, including how it might be conceptualized and pursued.

We see this book as one that will provide our professorial colleagues and graduate students with the content and questions to engage in an expanded discourse about the kinds of research that may proffer improved understanding of the nature of leadership, and that will lead to a more diverse and sensitive kind of educational institution than has been the case in the past.

The logic of the presentation of the chapters follows the idea of proximity to the 2002 *Scientific Research in Education* document, its content and perspective. Each subsequent chapter continues to touch upon the original publication by the NRC, but in an increasingly diverse and expanded scope. Here is a brief overview of each of the seven chapters.

Chapter 1 by Fenwick W. English, "The NRC's *Scientific Research in Education:* It Isn't Even Wrong!" includes a critique of the narrow scope of the NRC's work and offers counter assertions for each of the six of the NRC's maxims regarding "correct science." The chapter critiques the NRC's silence in regard to educational leadership and points out that scholarship that describes the development of leadership in the nation's military academies does not follow the precepts in the NRC report. The predominance of qualitative work in leadership is compelling testimony to the fact that greater understanding and new discoveries are not likely to be achieved with the kind of science proffered by the NRC, especially if leadership is democratic.

Chapter 2 by Linda C. Tillman, "Scientific Research on Education," explores the utility of the NRC's principles of scientific research in light of the increased use of racially and culturally sensitive research approaches in educational research. Specifically, Tillman makes a hypothetical assumption that all educational research is conducted based on the NRC principles. Given this hypothetical assumption, she discusses in what ways the principles are consistent or inconsistent with the criteria of Tillman's (2002) Culturally Sensitive Research Framework (CSRF). Using educational leadership as the field of inquiry, she provides examples of research on African Americans in school leadership that employ components of the CSRF and discusses to what extent the NRC principles are supported in the research.

Chapter 3 by Catherine A. Lugg and Carol F. Karpinski deals with the "Political Paradoxes of Scientific Research in Education." This chapter points out the political context in which the NRC worked, and how the Bush administration's emphasis on "scientific research" is contradicted by its retreat from actual scientific studies when the findings of them run a scupper of entrenched industrial interests. Support from the Protestant right groups for the Bush agenda is counterposed against the requirements in *Scientific Research in Education* for randomized field trials—a stipulation that experimenting in schools (and with children) is a legislated mandate. Other political issues are also highlighted in this chapter.

Chapter 4 by Gail C. Furman, "'Scientific' Research and the New Narrative for Educational Leadership," contrasts the "new" and "old" narratives regarding research in educational leadership. It traces the shifts in how leadership have been conceptualized and re-conceptualized, and indicates that ideas about research have not caught up with the "new" narrative about leadership. The "old" narrative has been deeply rooted in scientific management and "administrative science" and is grounded in notions of efficiency. The "new" narrative has been identified with specific "moral goods" such as learning for all children, social justice, and democratic community. This new perspective is grounded on the contextual richness and complexity of local school settings where leadership is a shared, distributed, and "constructed" phenomenon. In this "new" narrative seeking a definition of leadership practice that is generalizable across multiple school contexts is seen as futile.

Chapter 5 by Carolyn M. Shields, "What's a Researcher to Do? Insights for 'Post-Anything' Researchers" deals with the "posts" in education such as post-modernism, post-colonialism, post-structuralism, post-positivism, post-socialism, and post-foundationalism. Each of these perspectives offers a position which involves a denial of certitude. Such denials are contrasted against the early proponents of science and their works. Shields proposes a method to move the discourse forward, that of a dialogical participatory orientation advanced by Bakhtin in which "truth" is contained in the interaction and mutual reflection of all voices, avoiding the temptation to arrive at a forced consensus. Such a polyphonic method avoids both relativism and dogmatism. While this method proffers there are no absolutes, it doesn't mean there are no realities.

Chapter 6 by Michelle D. Young and Margaret Terry Orr, "Standards for Research(er) Integrity in Educational Leadership: Implications for Current and Future Researchers," makes the case that having standards such as those provided by the NRC benefits the field of educational research. However, Young and Orr also draw the reader's attention to what is missing within the NRC standards, namely the issue of research(er) integrity, as well as the need for broad interpretations of some elements of the standards. Subsequently, these authors present their own set of principles of research integrity, which center on objectivity, transparency and scrutiny. Young and Orr conclude with a discussion of implications for current practice and the preparation of future researchers in educational leadership.

Chapter 7 by Carolyn Riehl, "Research on Educational Leadership: Knowledge We Need for the World We Live In," juggles many of the ambiguities experienced by researchers in educational leadership with the ideas advanced in the NRC report. Riehl defends some aspects of the NRC's work by stressing that the core nature of science—evidence carefully gathered, interpreted, and made available for public scrutiny—is still worth pursuing, even though it does not encompass some knowledge-building efforts that may advance the field of leadership. The chapter encourages a more productive research enterprise by accepting the boundaries regarding different forms of scholarship and abandoning efforts to determine what counts as "science." The chapter concludes by positing that significant new research will develop knowledge by exploring leadership as a meaning-making social practice and by attending to the tasks of conceptual development, theory-building, and theory-testing, not just empirical evidence-gathering.

The ultimate determination of whether this book is valuable will be in the dialogue it provokes, in graduate classes, at research conferences, and in formulations and recommendations for future research about educational leadership and school administration. We are grateful for the many colleagues who offered their ideas and suggestions for a work like this. We are especially grateful for the support of the UCEA Executive Director, Michelle D. Young; Catherine A. Lugg, the UCEA Associate Director for Publications; the UCEA Executive Committee; and the UCEA Publications Committee.

1

The NRC's *Scientific Research in Education*: It Isn't Even Wrong

Fenwick W. English,
University of North Carolina at Chapel Hill

The Austro-American physicist and 1945 Nobel Laureate, Wolfgang Pauli, would sometimes dismiss scientific work he considered trivial or not positioned against the prevailing theories of the day with a derisive comment, "It isn't even wrong" (Begley, 2004, p. A7). Pauli's sentiments could be similarly advanced towards the National Research Council's (2002) work, *Scientific Research in Education*. Despite claims to the contrary, the NRC's agenda is to enshrine a Foucaldian "apparatus" in the form of "correct science" (Gordon, 1980, p. 132).

Such an apparatus would consist of an interlocking set of federal/private agencies which would privilege a certain form of knowing above all others and marginalize or dismiss the rest as unworthy of serious consideration and funding. Once established such a *regime of truth* works to become politically repressive to all other forms (Gordon, 1980, p. 133). From this perspective, St. Pierre's (2002) warning about such a regime of truth becoming enshrined as the universal standard in educational research is prescient, "The NRC Report should scare us all to death" (p. 27).

The purpose of this chapter is to critically examine the premises of the NRC's (2002) assertions and assumptions as they pertain to educational research in order to ascertain if their six guiding principles proffer the potential to advance our understanding of educational leadership. If not, then there is likely to be no new discoveries for understanding the importance of leadership in schools. The outcome is likely to be "same old, same old," for as Marcel Proust once said, "The voyage of discovery lies not in finding new landscapes . . . but in having new eyes" (Conord & Conord, 2002, p. 171). The NRC's six guiding principles are likely to ensure there will be no "new eyes" examining leadership or the role of leaders in schools.

THE EPITOME OF LOGICAL EMPIRICISM

The six standards for research set forth in the NRC report, which are called "a code of conduct" (p. 52) and represent the epitome of logical empiricism (Feyerabend, 1993, p. 157), are:

1. Pose significant questions that can be investigated empirically;
2. Link research to relevant theory;
3. Use methods that permit direct investigation of the question;
4. Provide a coherent and explicit chain of reasoning;
5. Replicate and generalize across studies;
6. Disclose research to encourage professional scrutiny and critique (NRC, 2002, p. 52).

Before accepting these criteria without scrutiny, it may be instructive to consider counter factuals and arguments which challenge them. This is especially important if we are concerned about whether their utilization will lead to any breakthrough discoveries ("new eyes") in understanding educational leadership or in much of education.

The underlying rationale supporting the NRC's (2002) document is that of Popperian rationality (pp. 16–17) regarding the growth of science and scientific knowledge as proceeding in a logical way of refutation and conjectures. However, as Lakatos (1999b) notes, "This is all logically possible: the only problem is that is has never happened in this way. So if we accept Popperian philosophy, then we also have to accept that the history of science is irrational, and that scientists have always behaved irrationally and immorally" (p. 98).

Lakatos (1999b) is correct as it pertains to discoveries. When Albert Einstein developed his famous equation $E = mc^2$, it had not been derived from years of working with numbers in physics labs. "Instead . . . he just spent a long time 'dreamily' thinking about light and speed and what was logically possible in our universe and what wasn't" (Bodanis, 2000, p. 80).

The history of scientific discoveries shows time and again that the discovery process is irrational, unpredictable, and rule independent. One example is Rontgen's discovery of X-rays (Gratzer, 2002, p. 12); the "magnetic moment" in quantum theory (Gratzer, 2002, p. 16). Indeed, one of the maxims of the famous Danish physicist and Nobel Prize winner Niels Bohr (1885–1962) was that good fundamental theories had to be "really crazy" and violate "common sense in a fundamental way" to be worth much (Gratzer, 2002, p. 42).

After the counterfactuals are presented for each of the NRC's six criteria for scientific research, the chapter examines the gap in them regarding educational leadership and the implications of this kind of structured silence. The chapter then posits why the codification of the rules of science are misguided and concludes with three major points in applying the NRC's criteria to a study of educational leadership.

NRC Assertion 1: Pose Significant
Questions That Can Be Investigated Empirically
Counter Assertion 1: Empiricism Is Not "Provable"
as the Basis for Determining Scientific Conduct

The NRC (2002) approach to the conduct of research in education is rooted in empiricism. As a doctrine embodying the research act, empiricism is a teleology, a self-affirming set of propositions regarding the nature of investigation, methods of proof, and a testing of relationships that are nested within one another. The first flaw in empiricism is that as an expression of a perspective, it is not empirical, that is, the legitimacy of empiricism cannot be established empirically.

Empiricism is a doctrine rooted in faith and it is a perspective that professes a logic within its own boundaries that is not open to dissent. The self-enclosed nature of empiricism, with its penchant for observation as the major form of verification, may shed some light on its weaknesses. The first guiding principle of the NRC's criteria for conducting scientific research is an insistence on framing a question which is deemed significant.

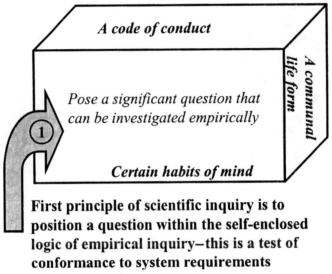

Figure 1.1 The Teleology of Empirical Investigations

What is a "significant" question is enclosed within a method. The method defines the nature of any question's importance. This is a teleology and is shown in Figure 1.1.

The NRC (2002) indicates that empiricism is essentially a "code of conduct" and represents "certain habits of mind" (p. 52). As a code of conduct, the mind set advanced is distinctively *normative*. It is represented in rules that govern behavior. This is entirely consistent with how Kuhn (1996) conceptualized "normal science" (p. 5). And despite the NRC's use of the concept of "open-minded thinking" (p. 53), a mind that works outside these habits would be subject to regulation and ridicule. "Openness" is entirely bound by the accepted habits of mind. As such, empiricism is subject to certain blind spots. It is unable to think outside its own self-imposed limitations. The "significant questions" are only those that can be approached by the nonempirically established "rules."

The definition of "discovery" is contained in the doctrine of empiricism. Nothing can be "discovered" (though it may be there or physically present) until it conforms to the logic of the system. Insisting upon empirical observation as the bedrock assumption for defining research does not insure its importance, nor does it proffer the grounds for "discovery."

As a perspective, empiricism will not consider any theory. Only those that are open to empirical probing are acceptable. For this reason, the theory of relativity, which came to Einstein in a dream, was nonempirical. Einstein had decided that even if an empirical experiment came back negative, "the experiment would be faulty — not his theory" (Aczel, 1999, p. 83).

The science proposed by the NRC (2002) is far from objective (p. 124). If one were to take all of the "six guiding principles" and apply them as rigorously as possible, one would still not have something scientific. In other words, if we included all of the six guiding principles of science we would still not have science itself because, "no single study or series of studies satisfy all of our guiding principles" (NRC, 2002, p. 79). If it is not possible for any study to satisfy all of the criteria, on what basis would a study be called "scientific"? The answer is "when those who call themselves scientists decide it is scientific" because "science is a communal form of life" (p. 53), and science is at its heart a "code of conduct" (p. 52) centered in "certain habits of mind" (p. 53). In this respect, what is scientific amount to determining who is faithful or not. It is a form of determining truth by consensus. The Kuhnian (1996) model of paradigm change summarized by Imre Lakatos (1999):

> For Kuhn scientific change — from one "paradigm" to another — is a mystical conversion which is not and cannot be governed by rules of reason and which falls totally within the realm of the (social) psychology of discovery. Scientific change is a kind of religious change. (p. 9)

If one were to apply all of the NRC's (2002) six guiding principles to a study or any series of studies and still have it not be "scientific," then there is no objective base (meaning one that can stand independently) for the establishment of science. If only the community of scientists finally has the determining say so, then what is "science" is subjectively determined by those already practicing science. This stand is consistent with the notion that empiricism is only conformance to a set of rules. What is true is simply a convention and what is science is determined by consensus. There is in this definition an embedded mysticism akin to religious orders. In the final analysis a Jesuit is only ordained by other Jesuits. Lakatos (1999) indicates: "If even in science there is no other way of judging a theory but by assessing the number, faith and vocal energy of its supporters then this must be even more so in the social sciences: truth lies in power" (p. 10).

The empiricism of the NRC (2002) is mystical not rational. Even after all of the "rules" have been followed one still does not have science, then science is not rational, nor is it dependent on the rules. The ultimate grounding of science is faith as determined by the faithful following. Feyerabend (1993) said it best when he remarked, "There is not a single rule that remains valid under all circumstances and not a single agency to which appeal can always be made" (p. 158).

> Finally, Albert Einstein was famous for his non-empirical "thought experiments." Once he imagined a circle spinning in space. The center of the circle did not move but its circumference was moving quickly in a circular direction. Einstein compared what happens in several reference frames . . . he concluded . . . that the boundary of the disk contracted as it spun . . . He deduced that in the presence of a gravitational force (or field), the geometry of space is non-Euclidean. (Aczel, 1999, p. 59)

One of the most serious criticisms of advancing logical empiricism as "correct science" is that it is blind to its own prejudices.

> Any science is based upon the special nature of that which it has made its object through its methods of objectifying. The method of modern science is characterized from the start by a refusal: namely to exclude all that which actually eludes its own methodology and procedures . . . Thus it gives the appearance of being total in its knowledge and in this way provides a defense behind which social prejudices and interests lie hidden and thus protected. (Gadamer, 1977, p. 93)

Barash (2003) indicates the same observation when he notes that:

> Science [is a] social and cultural enterprise, such that the questions asked by practicing scientists are unavoidably constrained by such factors as class, gender, the existing power structure (including, but not limited to, what is "fundable"), and . . . the existing scientific ethos. (p. B11)

NRC Assertion 2: Link Research to Relevant Theory
Counter Assertion 2: The Difference Between "Relevant" and "Non-Relevant" Theory Is Not Truthfulness but Power and Popularity

The second "guiding principle" of the NRC is that research must be linked to "relevant theory" (p. 59) because "... theory drives the research question, the use of methods, and the interpretation of results" (p. 62). The NRC claims that the use of its guiding principles will "help to distinguish science and nonscience" (p. 77).

At least one perspective on the utilization of theory in scientific investigations is that knowledge growth may actually be inhibited by a theoretical framework (Thomas, 1997).

> Theories can serve as totalizing discourses that limit vision, preserve the status quo, and prevent the kinds of eruptions of insight that tend to characterize knowledge growth in most fields. New Understandings typically arise from fragmented, local, and specific knowledge that is not tethered to the tenets of existing theory. Breakthroughs occur despite theory rather than because of it. (Riehl, Larson, Short, & Reitzug, 2000, p. 394)

Evidence on the nature of radical breakthroughs is noteworthy in the history of scientific discovery without the benefit of theory. Thomas Edison, who has held the record for the number of patents granted by the U.S. Patent Office, eschewed theory. "At the time I experimented on the incandescent lamp I did not understand Ohm's law," he said. "Moreover, I do not want to understand Ohm's law. It would prevent me from experimenting" (Conot, 1979, p. 133). Edison began his scientific work with what he described as the first step—"intuition." He was once asked by a new employee in his New Jersey laboratory what the rules were for working there. Edison spat tobacco on the floor and rasped, "Hell, there ain't no rules around here" (Conot, 1979, p. 386).

Karl Popper argued in 1934 that "the mathematical probability of all theories, scientific or pseudoscientific, given *any* amount of evidence is zero" (Lakatos, 1999, p. 3). Lakatos (1999) indicated that "scientific theories are not only equally unprovable but also equally improbable" (p. 3). Popper proposed a test which would be independent of any theory as opposed to being theory dependent: "A theory may be scientific even if there is not a shred of evidence in its favour. That is, the scientific or non-scientific character of a theory can be determined independently of the facts" (Lakatos, 1999, p. 3). To this end Popper proposed that the line of demarcation for claiming that one theory was scientific and the next one was not did not lie in a consensus of opinion, but rather in one that could specify in advance "a crucial experiment (or observation) which can falsify it" (Lakatos, 1999, p. 3). For a theory to claim to be scientific, the proponent had to be able to indicate an observation or a "crucial experiment" which would discredit it. Any proponent who failed to do so was dealing in a pseudo-scientific claim. Both Marxists and Freudians have consistently refused to engage in this critical demarcation. As it pertains to empiricism, what observable conditions or a crucial experiment would falsify empiricism? Would it be possible to find something which is true but not observable?

It ought to be clear that a "relevant" theory could indeed be false or pseudo-scientific. Empiricism defines "relevant" as socially acceptable because none of the criteria advocated by the NRC can stand independently as the hallmark of true science. Under this umbrella there can be no independent verification that the guidelines enclose exclusively.

Lakatos (1999) ascribes this state of affairs to the idea that there is or was ever any set of "facts" that could be proven from experiments. Propositions are indexed to other propositions, they are not derived from "facts" (p. 16). Theories contain sets of propositions and since all theories are proposition dependent, they are equally unprovable and inherently fallible. There is no line between scientific and non-scientific theories, or "relevant" and "non-relevant" theories which are provable or non-fallible because "all propositions of science are theoretical and incurably fallible" (p. 16). What is meant by "relevant" is "popular." It is nothing to do with a theory's independent "scientific" content or value. Insistence on linking investigations to "relevant theory" is way of perpetuating the current set of theories. Such a stance is anti-theoretical itself.

NRC Assertion 3: Use Methods That
Permit Direct Investigation of the Question
Counter Assertion 3: Methods Which Permit
Direct Investigation Reinforce Known Properties
and Theories and Impose a Limitation of Their Own

The ability to pre-specify one's methods is an expected aspect of scientific inquiry. Once again, while the logic of science indicates that the question should be developed first and then an appropriate method(s) selected secondly (NRC, 2002, p. 63), in some cases methods or apparatuses dictate the kinds or ranges of questions that are possible to pursue (Kuhn, 1996, p. 27). Significant questions are shaped by available methods. They do not stand independently apart from them. There are also other reasons where the strength of a "direct investigation" is compromised (NRC, 2002, p. 66).

The prespecification of methods of direct investigation reinforce known relationships, and while they might lead to discerning a new phylum of tiny creatures living on the mouthparts of lobsters via a hand lens and a light microscope as an exemplar cited by the NRC (2002, p. 63), no new theories were part of the "discovery," nor was the theory in use able to predict the presence of such rotifer-like creatures.

Some very important theories being considered today are not only non-empirical, but are likely never to lead to any direct observation possibilities. For example, string theory, the idea that beyond electrons and quarks, "every particle is composed of a tiny filament of energy, some hundred billion times smaller than a single atomic nucleus . . . which is shaped like a little string" (Greene, 2004, p. 18) are likely never to be observed. "Strings are so small that a direct observation would be tantamount to reading the text on this page from a distance of 100 light-years: it would require resolving power nearly a billion times finer than our current technology allows" (Greene, 2004, p. 352).

Should work involving string theory be subsequently abandoned? Should the lack of observable manifestations lead to research with only observable manifestations? While the answer is most likely negative, one can be sure that if the NRC followed its own guidelines it wouldn't recognize it or fund it. Yet many physicists believe that string theory will provide the basis for Einstein's unified theory that would combine general relativity and quantum mechanics into a single theory.

Then, of course, there is the matter of Theodor Kaluza, an obscure German mathematician that in 1919 proposed to Einstein that space contained a fourth dimension that nobody had ever seen (Greene, 2004, p. 360). His assertion was purely imaginary. Extending Einstein's general theory of relativity to a higher scope, he discovered that an extra equation that he derived contained Maxwell's description of electromagnetic fields. Without benefit of any observation, Kaluza had produced "a framework that combined Einstein's original equations of general relativity with those of

Maxwell's equations of electromagnetism," one of the most critical issues in physics at the time (Greene, 2004, p. 361). Here was a truly significant problem resolved by imagination.

Using Kaluza's insights, physicists today have sketched out the probable shape of space with six dimensions. These have never been observed. They are reachable only mathematically. At least in physics, limiting problem solving only to methods that permit direct observation would put an end to what many physicists believe is "the key to resolving some of the universe's deepest mysteries" (Greene, 2004, p. 374).

NRC Assertion 4: Provide a
Coherent and Explicit Chain of Reasoning
Counter Assertion 4: Explicit Chains of
Reasoning Are Rarely the Stuff of Discoveries

The NRC (2002) insists that without tight linkages between reasoning and evidence interconnected to theory that characterizes "rigorous research," rival hypotheses cannot adequately be dealt with and other forms of biases may enter in and skew results. Once again, when a researcher is working within known parameters it is possible to specify in advance the assumptions, the conditions, the methods and deal with alternative interpretations. However, these aspects would never have led to some of the most important breakthroughs in medicine such as the discovery of penicillin or cortisone. These breakthroughs were "out of paradigm" at the time as nearly all medical discoveries have been. No amount of the extant scientific reasoning or guiding principles would have produced them (see LeFanu, 1999, p. 218).

One of the problems highlighted by Edward DeBono (1972) is that while the requirement for logical thinking is important to understand a discovery, logical thinking would not have resulted in the discovery. Some things are logical only retrospectively because as DeBono (1972) points out, "yes-no" systems of thought or logic "preserves ideas and is of no help in changing them—it has no creative ability whatsoever" (p. 30) because logic exists with "boxed definitions" that are geared to what is known and "make the evolution of ideas impossible since an idea cannot drift in or out of a definition but must at all times be inside or outside" (p. 31). Clear understandings are often not part of medical discovery as well (see LeFanu, 1999).

And LeFanu (1999) indicates that there are many things in use in medicine today for which there is no explicit chain of reasoning which explains them (pp. 206, 340). Should we stop using them because medical researchers and doctors are not able to "provide coherent, explicit chains of reasoning"? If the principles elucidated by the NRC did not lead to their discovery and further can't explain how they work, how inclusive are these guiding principles? LeFanu (1999) quotes Philip Gell, Emeritus Professor of genetics at the University of Birmingham:

> The heart of the problem lies in the fact that we are dealing not with a chain of causation but with a network that is a system like a spider's web in which a perturbation at any point of the web changes the tension of every fibre right back to its anchorage in the blackberry bush. The gap in our knowledge is not merely unbridged, but in principle unbridgeable and our ignorance will remain ineluctable. (p. 278)

NRC Assertion 5: Replicate and Generalize Across Studies
Counter Assertion 5: Replication Across Studies Leads to
Context Free Generalizations: Especially Dangerous
in Understanding Effective Leadership

Early efforts to produce leaders via institutionalized means led to the incorporation of methods and structuring curricula so as to produce generalizable results that were not context dependent. One example is the creation in European nations and the United States of military academies whose purpose was to prepare military officers for combat. The error of their ways was soon apparent as noted by John Keegan (1987) who remarked, "The generalship of one age and place may not at all resemble that of another . . . context . . . is all" (pp. 1, 3).

The current dilemma with creating standards for educational leaders has led to the same results (English, 2003). When roles are standardized for purposes of measuring the worth of preparation programs via accreditation, then schools and schooling contexts are likewise standardized. In a quest for generalization across all possible circumstances, job complexity and competence intertextualized with situations are erased. Generic principles are only helpful with generic challenges. One study of executive leadership refers to such a posture as the role of an "orthodox

innovator" (Skowronek, 2002, p. 88). The dilemma of the "orthodox innovator" is that he/she only sees change from the path which was already
traced and has to project leadership on the grounds that will be in con-
formity with past traditions. To severely challenge such traditions would
be self-defeating and call the credibility of the leader into question. The
"orthodox-innovator" conceptualizes change purely within the bounded
rationality of what is already known. On a scale of zero to ten in "discovery," the orthodox innovator might be one-to-two. Such orthodox
change is one of the reasons Seymour Sarason (1990) took note of how
schools continue to fail to change in predictable ways. Fundamental axioms are rarely challenged.

NRC Assertion 6: Disclose Research to
Encourage Professional Scrutiny and Critique
Counter Assertion 6: The Disclosure of Research to
Encourage Professional Scrutiny and Critique Is No
Guarantee of Success or Acceptance, Especially with "New Eyes"

While it is a commonly accepted canon of public science that one must
share results and open one's research to scrutiny, the disclosure of such information is no guarantee that the truth will prevail. The process of science is superficially rational, but always deeply human and laced with the
foibles of human nature. Personal jealousies and feuds and prejudices of
all kinds dot the scientific landscape, from Poincare's sulkings (Bodanis,
2000, p. 78) to the professional scalding of Barbara McClintock, the Nobel Prize winning geneticist who asserted the view that genes within ge-
netic structure were not stable.

In 1951 Barbara McClintock gave a symposium for colleagues in Cold
Spring Harbor New York. As usual, her presentation was laced with statistics and extensive data sets, all the accoutrements of the NRC's bench-
marks of scientific research. But her talk failed to provoke anything such
as a rational response in the scientific community:

> Scientists scrambling to learn molecular biology wanted it simple; they did
> not like a genetic system that was fluid, moving, changing, and intricately
> regulated. They reacted with puzzlement, frustration, even hostility. "I don't
> want to hear a thing about what you're doing. It may be interesting, but I

understand it's kind of mad," a biologist told her. A leading molecular biologist called her "just an old bag who'd been hanging around Cold Spring Harbor for years." (McGrayne, 1993, p. 168)

McClintock published her work in a lengthy article in 1953. When only three colleagues requested copies, she concluded that publishing was a waste of time and stopped giving seminars at Cold Spring Harbor about her work (McGrayne, 1993, p. 168).

The NRC (2002) presents the image of science as supremely rational. Facts, figures, and data presented logically are made to appear as if they will be persuasive if made public and open to criticism. The history of scientific breakthroughs presents another picture, however. While verification of existing theories is popular and more acceptable, true discovery ("new eyes") is often ignored, discouraged, or ridiculed. Public scrutiny is no guarantor that scientific discoveries will be honored, and many scientific breakthroughs have laid fallow for years because of the lack of objectivity and rationality within the scientific community to honor its own tenets. Take the case of Subrahmanyan Chandrasekhar, who at the tender age of nineteen advanced the notion that matter in the universe must collapse under great pressure which created denser masses. This discovery was derided by the leading astrophysicists of the day, but is accepted and known as the "Chandrasekhar limit" (Chandrasekhar, 1995, p. 97). Similar scorn was heaped upon Gerard de Vaucouleurs who hypothesized that the galaxies were grouped into superclusters along fault lines created by gravity. Despite meticulous data gathering, de Vaucouleurs was considered a crackpot (Mcg. Thomas, 1995, p. A12).

The NRC is also naive in assuming that researchers will always want to make their research and data public. What if they don't? There are several high profile cases of researchers failing to show their data to back up their assertions. This often happens when the subject of the research has become politicized. The first concerns global warming. A distinguished climate researcher, Michael Mann, put together a graph that shows that average temperatures since 1900 have been escalating. The shape of the global warming resembles a hockey stick and was named the "hockey stick" graph. The graph has been used extensively to support the idea that fossil fuels are changing the earth's average temperatures. But the hockey stick graph has been challenged as employing flawed methods that yield next to useless information. The charge has been made that analytical methods employed would nearly always produce a hockey stick, even if the data were selected at random (Regalado, 2005, p. A13). These allegations were made by a non-scientist and after initially providing the critic with some data regarding his hockey stick, Dr. Mann cut him off and refused to release his computer codes which constructed it.

The second example concerns a controversial concept in education regarding "value added assessment" made famous by Sanders and Horn (1998) in Tennessee. The TVAAS (Tennessee Value Added Assessment System) ostensibly provides a method for paying teachers based on their students' progress on standardized tests. The value added system is supposed to factor out the effects of the students' socioeconamic status (SES) that has been shown to skew test results. A close study by Kupermintz (2003) using some of the TVAAS data casts serious doubt on the claims of the TVAAS. Kupermintz (2003) reviewed the assertions by the proponents of TVAAS and challenged the claim that SES and prior achievement could be divorced or "blocked" from calculating the effects of the teacher on student achievement (p. 295). The claims by those of the TVAAS cry for a fair and urgent examination of all the data and the methods used to produce it. Kupermintz (2003) observes:

> To date, numerous requests by the author for access to the TVAAS data have been met with blank refusals . . . Education researchers . . . and organizations such as the Carnegie Foundation have requested data directly from Sanders only to be turned down or stalled . . .

The process of politicization interferes with the free flow of information identified as crucial by the NRC. And large clinical field trials are no guarantee that the situation could or would be improved.

> Massive clinical trials, testing out new drugs or treatment methods, have long been the one type of biomedical team science . . . They are expensive, decentralized, difficult to supervise, and effectively impossible to replicate . . . In short, large clinical trials invite sloppiness and cheating. (Judson, 2004, p. 296)

A third example is much closer to home. In the spring of 2005, Arthur Levine, President of Teachers College, Columbia University released a scathing report on the situation confronting educational leadership programs. Based largely on survey research in which faculty response rates were quite low (36–39%), educational leadership programs were described as sporting an irrelevant curriculum, low admission and graduation standards, a weak faculty not producing much scholarship, were disconnected from practice and staffed by many adjuncts and possessed inadequate clinical experiences (Levine, 2005). The report explains that there were site visitations to twenty-eight schools and departments of education. The reader is never informed where the sites were, except two schools were exempted from the damning indictment of all programs. This is a flagrant example of where information is withheld from a discerning reader. Where were these places? Were the faculty given an opportunity to respond to the observations and conclusions? How was the accuracy confirmed? The reader is never given information about which sites possessed which shortcomings on which criteria. What is provided are anecdotal narratives. In short, there is no independent way anybody can verify Levine's (2005) conclusions based on site visitation data, a stunning rejection of the NRC's criterion regarding disclosure of scientific research.

THE NRC'S SILENCE ON EDUCATIONAL LEADERSHIP

Although the NRC report (2002) speaks to the necessity for competent leadership in creating a scientific culture in a federal research agency (p. 132), and recognizes it as a source of influence in complex educational systems (p. 84), it is silent on matters of research pertaining to educational administration. In fact, school leaders are not even cited in the scope of human volition in schools when the NRC says, "Education is centrally concerned with people: learners, teachers, parents, citizens, and policy makers" (p. 86). The roles of school administrators apparently do not exist in the NRC's view of human decision making, except as something to consider in how "programs are implemented in diverse educational settings" (p. 125). Presumably this might include a school principal or superintendent, but it is not really clear whether in the NRC's opinion it is important at all except as an issue regarding the fidelity of implementation of a selected research design. Maxwell (2004) similarly comments that human beliefs, values and volition are primarily considered "in terms of their effect on the education research enterprise, rather than as an integral part of the phenomena studied" (p. 7).

Thus, the silence on school leadership is ominous. As a variety of research studies in education are cited that meet some of the NRC's six guiding principles, we are presented with exemplars regarding class size research as being superior because it involved randomized field trials (NRC, 2002, pp. 64–65); college women's career choices because it utilized more than one theoretical models (NRC, 2002, p. 107); teacher salaries and student dropout rates as how the power of causal attribution could be enhanced through model elimination using an explicit hypothesis (NRC, 2002, p. 116); comparisons of catholic schools and public schools involving a search for a mechanism by which the former attained "an equitable social distribution of academic achievement" (NRC, 2002, pp. 118–89); and elementary school students and learning ratio and proportion based on a good deal of previous literature regarding mathematical ideas and teaching approaches (p. 121). This latter exemplar was highlighted because "it involved research within the complex interactions of teachers and students and allowed the everyday demands and opportunities of schooling to affect the investigation" (NRC, 2002, p. 122).

Not only are there no exemplars regarding what role, if any, leadership plays in conducting such experiments in schools, but the implicit role of the school leader in these scenarios is relegated to that of a variant of an agricultural extension agent working with farmers (teachers) to faithfully implement research "proven" strategies that produce the "best" crops (student learning) on extant soils. The role of the school administrator is by default locked into one of an antiseptic factotum who should get out of the way and not become a contaminant as the process of "objective science" unfolds, despite the fact that the Southern Regional Education Board (2004) reported that research conducted by Kenneth Leithwood at the University of Toronto concluded that "the principal's leadership accounts for about 20 percent of the school's impact on student achievement" (p. 1).

One would hope that NRC's failure to account for the impact of leadership as an independent variable was simply an oversight, but the frozen silences contained in the NRC's presentation of correct science, its identified methods, purposes, exemplars, and principles derived from a never named "common conceptual frame" (NRC, 2002, p. 151; St. Pierre, 2002,

p. 26) offer no counter-factuals to its hegemony. "That frame . . . is clearly some form of positivism. Only a single kind of science will be advanced with such practices" (St. Pierre, 2004, p. 26). It is to the detriment of any study of educational leadership that the dominant positivist traditions in research in the field which have been universally criticized as containing intellectual and conceptual blind spots (Heck & Hallinger, 1999, pp. 141–162) are almost certainly going to be reinforced by the NRC's guiding principles. It would certainly be ironic that in the name of improving research standards in educational leadership, we actually create a situation where it is nearly impossible to advance any new understanding at all.

IMPLICATIONS FOR THE STUDY OF LEADERSHIP

When applied to a study of educational leadership, the six guiding principles advanced by the NRC are disturbing. One avenue of human inquiry has been privileged above all others, delegitimatizing the remainder as "not science" and therefore not worthy to be funded, not by the federal government anyway.

Johnson (1996) indicates that leadership has been treated as an empirical phenomenon, "conductive to study from a descriptive, social scientific, and value-free standpoint" (p. 13). He notes that when leadership is defined in this manner, it is the focus of study from "methods of sociology, psychology, and political science (among others)" (p. 13). However, Johnson explains that leadership is also "an inherently humanistic concern whose ambiguities, contextuality, and normativity require the interpretive methods and devices of history, literature, and philosophy (among others" (p. 13). Johnson (1996) cautions,

> No account of leadership can be complete, or completely adequate, unless it makes some explicit attempt to integrate these two methodological perspectives. The challenge in trying to effect a more synoptic view of leadership revolves around the question of what to do with the ethical or moral aspects of leadership practice. (p. 14)

John Dewey's (1929) essay, "The Sources of a Science of Education" are instructive here. Dewey observed, "Education is a mode of life, of action.

As an act it is wider than science" (p. 75). However, Dewey's observation has been ignored by the NRC as it privileges the first venue of research (empiricism) for the study of leadership even as prominent sociologist Michael Mann counsels, "No laws are possible in sociology . . . for the number of cases is far smaller than the number of variables effecting the outcome" (as cited in McLemme, 2004, p. A10).

This observation would certainly be applicable to a study of educational leadership. The NRC and its advocates have very little to say about the study of leadership. Rather, leadership is assumed to be present in order to implement the empirical, randomized field trial results regarding educational methods and means. Thus, the implicit logic goes, when randomized field trials show a particular method of reading to be superior, the educational leader simply implements it in the schools. The yoking of educational leadership to such clinical trials assumes that (a) leaders come to office without other political motives or agendas that are not driven by science, and (b) the decision-making processes are nearly devoid of political influence other than be driven by the results of such trials. Furthermore, when various pressures are placed on educational office holders, they can prevail by quoting or citing definitive research results from randomized field trials. While such politically pristine situations may be present in monasteries, laboratories or hospitals, they are rarely present in schools.

The naiveté of the proponents of randomization and scientific-based research as they define it, make a strong case for "engineering research" (Burkhardt & Schoenfeld, 2003, p. 3). In this approach the argument is presented that "engineering research" includes the concept of *cumulativity*, "a growing core of results, developed through studies that build upon previous work, which are accepted by both the research community and the public as reliable and non-controversial within a well-defined range of circumstances" (Burkhardt & Schoenfield, 2003, p. 6).

Unlike medical research where the public may be interested only in which treatments are best, the public in public education are not disinterested patrons who await objectively to hear the words of experts. Parents in public schools act in ways that reproduce social inequity. Forms of inequity embodied in tracking plans and programs for the gifted and talented are designed to reproduce social inequities and privilege (Apple, 1982; Oakes, 1985; Sapon-Shevin, 1994; Spring, 1976, 1989). Schools are social sorting machines (Katz, 1968; Spring, 1976, 1989) and research that exposes the influence of social elites and the ways schools operate to conform to give children "what they deserve" will be stoutly resisted, attacked and ignored. "Scientific based research" is unlikely to expose, probe or be welcomed in such situations. But these circumstances are precisely the ones that educational leaders know first hand as volatile and political dynamite. As Klinker and Hackmann (2004) observe, "The decision-making process is reflective of societal values, yet is intensely personal. Going against a cultural value takes courage, and such decisions are not made without personal cost" (p. 452).

So when the NRC (2002) warns that, "the major weakness of nonrandomized designs is selectivity bias—the counter-interpretation that the treatment did not cause the difference in outcomes, but, rather, unmeasured prior existing differences (differential selectivity) between the groups did" (p. 113), one has to smile. What we have here is a rather interesting description of the perils of democratic leadership. When a leader is selected by democratic means, we have a nonrandomized design which exhibits selectivity bias. School leaders are not chosen nor continued in office by random means. Rather, leadership selection is a complicated and complex sociopolitical process involving transactions with commonly held cultural symbols embedded in stories or narratives (Gardner, 1995, p. 14). These stories need "to be yoked to specific messages . . . that can direct and guide an inner circle and a wider polity" (Gardner, 1995, p. 16). In a society driven by economic interests the ascension to positions of power is anything but random, and the forces at play ensure it is highly selective (biased), the kind of situational stability that requires conditions ". . . when a causal question is simple, sharply focused and easily justified" (Cook, 2002, p. 179). Such necessary theoretical stability has been described as a recipe:

> It seeks to describe the consequences of a set of activities that can be listed as though they were recipe ingredients and can be actively manipulated as a whole to ascertain what effects the lumped manipulation has. The aim is to describe the effects of a given cause, to test whether a treatment is effective. (Cook, 2002, p. 179)

Cook (2002) also indicates that the conditions in which the recipe theory would apply are not stringent enough because they may contain "hidden casual contingencies" (p. 179). He then indicates what would be necessary to correct or ameliorate them:

> So, a second understanding of causation requires specifying all the contingencies (co-causes) that impact on an effect, including those that follow from a causal manipulation but are prior to the effect basic research places a high premium on learning why a particular cause is effective and what all the other causes of a particular effect are. (Cook, 2002, p. 179)

It seems clear from these descriptions that the kind of controls that "scientific research" requires to be "evidence-based" would necessitate a form of leadership selection and study of those in leadership positions (as well as their simplest decisions that could be reduced to recipe formula), might only be met with research on Queen Victoria (1837–1901) or stable dictatorships such as Portugal's Antonio Salazar (1932–1968) or Spain's caudillo Francisco Franco (1939–1975). The fact is that research design purity requires a kind of situational solidity and decision locus simplicity that few, if any, school superintendents or principals enjoy or would even recognize today. The job is highly complex, political, multi-dimensional, involves contradictions and tensions reflective of life in a democracy that produces high levels of job anxiety and stress (see Ackerman & Maslin-Ostrowski, 2002; Beatty, 2000; Fenwick, 2000; Gilman & Lanman-Givens, 2001; Glass, Bjork & Brunner, 2000; Lam, 1984; Lindle, 2004; Patterson, 2000).

The difficulty in approaching a study of leadership using the NRC criteria is found in Phillips and Loy's (2003) *Character in Action: The U.S. Coast Guard on Leadership* and Johnson and Harper's (2005) *Becoming a Leader the Annapolis Way*. The U.S. Government spends millions of dollars on leadership in its military academies and Reserve Officer Training Corps (ROTC) efforts. Phillips and Loy (2003) text they lay out the twelve principles that define the culture that produces leaders. As Phillips and Loy (2003) state, "The academy exists to shape leaders, and those who graduate, without exception, are expected to become leaders" (p. 20). A close examination of the principles shows statements such as, "Make your organization like a family—a group of people taking care of one another," and "Create an organization of doers where everybody works at maximum speed and efficiency" (p. 17). Johnson and Harper (2005) proffer twelve combat lessons from the navy's leadership laboratory (the Naval Academy). The lessons from Annapolis include, "follow first," "the crucible of character," "create tri-level vision," "inoculate for stress," and "lead by example."

These lessons, maxims or axioms are never connected to any of the NRC's six guiding principles. None of the Coast Guard's twelve principles nor the Navy's twelve combat lessons are connected to formal empirical testing, linked to any stipulated relevant theory, produced by methods that permitted direction investigation of the principles, delineated by explicit chains of reasoning, identified as being the result of replicated studies, or subjected to rigorous scientific scrutiny. Using the NRC's criteria for "scientific research," the U.S. Coast Guard's leadership preparation program described by Phillips and Loy (2003) and Johnson and Harper's (2005) learning to lead via the Annapolis way, are decidedly unscientific. It would be an example of what Cook (2002) has described as the product of "the enlightenment model" (p. 190). Such an approach:

> involves information blended from existing theories, personal testimony, extrapolations from surveys, the consensus of a field, empirical claims from experts who may or may not have interests to defend, and novel concepts that are au courant and broadly applied—like social capital is in sociology and political science today. (p. 190)

Cook's (2002) criticism of the "enlightenment model" is similar to English's (2004a) critiquing of the use of the Interstate School Leaders Licensure Consortium (ISLLC) standards in educational administration. While Cook (2002) is primarily concerned about the lack of "special privilege to science in general or to experiments in particular" (p. 190), English (2004a) has been concerned that the ISLLC standards have been paraded as science, but lack an independent measure of their truthfulness beyond popularity. Both are concerned about how claims of efficacy are to be substantiated. Neither the U.S. government nor the accreditation boards live up to the NRC's guidelines, and even when empirical methods have been applied to the study of leadership, the results have been disappointing.

Maxwell (2004) has differentiated between variance theory and process theory. This distinction appears especially significant when studying leadership where sociopolitical factors are not noise to be controlled, but interactive in context to be understood. Variance theory seeks to control contextual factors that impinge on the ability to stipulate generalizations largely derived from quantitative approaches. What is desired are statements that are invariant and independent of context. Process theory, on the other hand, deals with "events and the processes that connect them" where what is studied are the linkages in situ. And these are contextually open to investigation with a different methodology and epistemology. While the NRC (2002) insists that there are no differences between qualitative and quantitative research methods when it is rigorous (p. 67), they end up imposing variance theory on all research along with an implicit hierarchy of research methods in which context revealed in qualitative inquiry attempting to discern particular situations or context is subordinated to quantitative notions of linear causality as denoted in patterns (Maxwell, 2004, pp. 8–9). And St. Pierre (2002) asserts that "The NRC report is shockingly silent about its epistemological allegiance" (p. 26).

The impact of the application of variance theory on dynamic contexts has been to reduce the leader and the leadership locus to simplistic codes in order to come to grips with any idea of what is actually occurring. Variance theory as a methodological approach has reduced leadership to impersonal actions sketched out on remarkably uniform canvas, all imbued with the pigment of the structural-functionalistic theoretical frame. In a quest for generalizable behaviors across context free settings, leadership has been reduced to near meaningless globs of undifferentiated paint. For example, in the most recent and popular version of effective leadership, leader acts are reduced to five generic patterns (Kouzes & Posner, 1987). The patterns depend upon a universe in which context is either irrelevant or optional. They have been clumped together into: (a) Challenging the Process; (b) Inspiring a Shared Vision; (c) Enabling Others to Act; (d) Modeling the Way; and (e) Encouraging the heart (pp. 310–311). Such views of leadership are formulaic and prescriptive, yet lack any predictability, one of the hallmarks of scientific theory. Such studies invariably involve a kind of double bind logic highlighted by Lakatos (1999) as a weakness of social science theory development, that is, the problem of *inductivism*.

For a theory to be predictive instead of prescriptive and normative, it cannot use the same facts twice, once in the creation of the theory and then to validate it as truthful (Lakatos, 1999b, p. 111). This is a perennial problem in creating social science theories which turn out to be correlative but not predictive. And it exerts a peculiarly devilish twist when a claimed causal relationship vanishes in a definitional primordial ooze. Kupermintz (2003) called such a relationship into question when he noted that in the TVAAS claims of teacher effects that "the single largest factor affecting academic growth of populations of students is differences in effectiveness of individual classroom teachers" (Sanders, 1988):

> The statement appears to imply that there are two distinct variables—teacher effectiveness and differences in student learning—and that the former causes the latter. Unfortunately, such causal interpretation is faulty because teacher effectiveness is defined and measured by the magnitude of student gains. In other words, differences in student learning determines—by definition—teacher effectiveness; a teacher whose students achievement is larger gains the "effective teacher." (Kupermintz, 2003, p. 289)

The NRC (2002) insists that all of science is the same, no matter what field is involved. From one perspective the statement is undoubtedly true. Empiricism can be applied to all fields. Yet, As Figure 1.2 illustrates, the social sciences have had unique problems not affiliated with the physical sciences, namely what Habermas (1981) has referred to as a double hermeneutic task in which the social scientist enters into

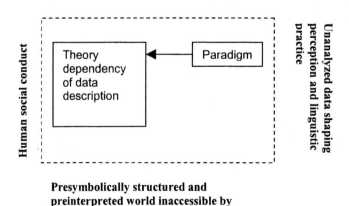

Presymbolically structured and preinterpreted world inaccessible by observation

Figure 1.2.   The "Double Bind Hermeneutical" Dilemma of the Social Scientist After Habermas

discussions that are not only theory and paradigm dependent, but rest on a preinterpreted world that functions below "the threshold of theory construction" (p. 110).

This everyday experience is "already symbolically structured and inaccessible to mere observation" (Habermas, 1981, p. 110). Thus, the social scientist is confronted with a meaning frame in which he is immersed, but is trying to objectively enter and understand human social conduct. Any claim of neutrality must bring with it an attempt to understand this pretheoretical, unanalyzed world in which all humans swim, but of which many are unaware. If social science fails to deal with its own nonobservable and nonempirical base, it cannot do what it professes to do, namely engage in scientific work as defined by the NRC's (2002) six guiding principles.

The predilection for sweeping generalizations across leadership contexts in the search for parsimony has produced very little in the way of understanding regarding the peculiarities of leadership, and no theory has so far been advanced in educational administration that has exhibited a proclivity to be predictive, especially when novel events are concerned. Heilbrunn (1996) has summarized this point:

> The scientific quest for a generic model of leadership can take one only so far. Employing factor analysis to quantify leadership and focusing so minutely on the qualities of leadership, the field repeatedly loses sight of one of the principal reasons for its subject's essentially unpredictable nature—the environment in which leader's function. Or, to put it another way, leadership studies lacks an adequate concern for context, historical or situational. (p. 8)

The point made by Heilbrunn (1996) that more contextually centered research is required in leadership applies to the apparent success of Stephen Skowronek (2002) of Yale. Skowronek's work predicted the kind of crisis in the presidency that marked Bill Clinton's impeachment, and a situation where George Bush would press for a war someplace (Valelly, 2003, p. B10). Yet Skowronek's theory has not enjoyed respectability among some political scientists because it ". . . doesn't have the right 'look'" (p. B10). Skowronek's methods were historical and qualitative and therefore not "real science"—"work that requires lots of data, big computer runs, formal modeling, and regular National Science Foundation funds" (p. B12). Yet Skowronek's work has been able to become predictive without the benefit of the kind of quantitative number crunching used as examples in the NRC report.

Another example of historical and qualitative insight exemplifying Maxwell's (2004) position in the key strength of qualitative research (p. 8) has been supplied by Pulitzer Prize winning biographer Robert Caro (2002) in his work *The Years of Lyndon Johnson: Master of the Senate*. In painstaking detail, Caro outlines the qualities of legislative leadership and the transformation of the "master of the senate" which resulted in the passage of the nation's first civil rights bill:

> So Lyndon Johnson changed—and changed the course of American history. For at last this leader of men would be leading, fighting, not only, for himself but for a great cause. This man who in the pursuit of his aims could be so utterly ruthless—who would let nothing stand in his way; who, in the pursuit, deceived, and betrayed and cheated—would be deceiving and betraying and cheating on behalf of something other than himself: specifically, on behalf of the sixteen million Americans whose skins were dark. (p. 862)

Caro (2002) then lays out his details in a compelling narrative that explains more about legislative leadership than any variance theory centered study could include:

> By grasping in a moment, on the Senate floor, the possibilities of Clint Anderson's amendment; by seizing that moment before it could vanish from the floor; by delicately adding jury trail amendment after jury trial amendment until he finally had the amendment that would attract enough votes to let the bill pass, he had displayed a mastery of small-scale, intricate legislative maneuver. In a republic, which had, during the past century of its existence, grown accustomed to thinking of governmental leadership almost solely in terms of executive leadership, he had provided a vivid demonstration of the potentialities of legislative leadership. A master of a profession cannot but know he is a master, cannot but feel joy and pride in exercising that master . . . the common ground on which he had at last brought both sides together was not ground he had discovered, but ground he had created. (p. 1004)

Caro (2002) quotes C. Vann Woodward as saying of Johnson's achievement, "The air of compromise is rarely appreciated fully by men of principle" (p. 1005).

The complex personality of Lyndon Johnson and coming to grasp his approach to legislative leadership depends upon a careful reconstruction of the man and his context for leading. And it involves recognizing "the reality and importance of meaning, as well as of physical and behavioral phenomena, as having explanatory significance, and the essentially *interpretative* nature of . . . understanding the former" (Maxwell, 2004, p. 8).

Caro (2002) documents how Johnson moved among men. Lyndon Johnson, says Caro (2002), knew how to read men. "He had the genius for studying a man and learning his strengths and weaknesses and hopes and fears, his deepest strengths and weaknesses; what it was that the man wanted—not what he said he wanted but what he *really* wanted—and what it was that the man feared, *really* feared" (p. 136). After interviewing those who worked with Johnson, Caro (2002) says: "He read with a novelist's sensitivity, with an insight that was unerring, with an ability, shocking in the depth of its penetration and perception, to look into a man's heart and know his innermost worries and desires" (p. 136).

It was from this ability acquired early on in Johnson's political career that he worked his way through the Senate and pieced together the compromise that would be startling. Lyndon Johnson knew how to listen. As Caro (2002) describes how Johnson worked behind the scenes "listening, listening to what they were saying, and listening to what they weren't saying. And out of the buttonholing, and the asking, and the listening, Lyndon Johnson was beginning to form a strategy. For as he listened, he heard something" (p. 890).

What Lyndon Johnson heard was what the Southern Senators were not telling him, namely, that while they were opposed to a broad range of civil rights for African Americans (in housing, economic benefits, etc.), they were not opposed for them to vote. Even Strom Thurmond from South Carolina did not use the word "never" when faced with this issue (Caro, 2002, p. 891). From this hiatus in Southern opposition, Johnson created the "space" to pass a civil rights bill because he reasoned that once African Americans had the right to vote, they could end other forms of discrimination at the ballot box (Caro, 2002, p. 892).

As one reads Caro's (2002) *The Years of Lyndon Johnson: Master of the Senate*, it becomes clear how Lyndon Johnson led in the senior chamber of the U.S. government, and how he was responsible for passage of the first civil rights bill since the Civil War and its aftermath. It is also clear how the kinds of empiricism and investigation proffered by the NRC would fall so miserably short of the mark in a study of Johnson's leadership. Adhering to the six guidelines for scientific research in education would considerably reduce the scope and range of Caro's (2002) portrait of Lyndon Johnson. The requirement to "replicate and generalize across studies" can be seen as a tool to erase context. All legislative contexts are not the same. Laws are the product of compromises over specific issues and interests. Other requirements from the NRC such as linking research to relevant theory and the mandate to construct procedures to enable replicating and generalizing across studies would also work against the construction of the rich detail that creates the database to understand Johnson's complex legislative leadership. Johnson's rise to power as a politician was anything but a random process, and the idea of doing field trials are simply unworkable. Paul Feyerabend (1993) perhaps summarized it best when he observed:

> Today knowledge is quantitative and theoretical, at least as far as our leading natural scientists are concerned. Who is right? That depends on what kind of information has privileged status, and this in turn depends on the culture, or the "cultural leaders" who use the information. Many people, without much thought, prefer technology to harmony with Nature; hence, quantitative and theoretical information is regarded as "read" and qualities as "apparent" and secondary. But a culture that centres on humans, prefers personal acquaintance to abstract relations (intelligence quotients; efficiency statistics) and a naturalists' approach to that of molecular biologists will say that knowledge is qualitative and will interpret quantitative laws as bookkeeping devices, not as elements of reality. (p. 236)

Applied to a study of leadership, the NRC's (2002) admonitions and norms will result in the same kinds of results that have characterized the study of leadership today. In short, the application of the NRC's (2002) criteria are profoundly anti-change in advancing a course of action that proffers any "discoveries" in studies of leadership. What we will have are more types of "verification" of what is already known.

The impact of the continuation of field trials using randomization has not served medicine well either. James LeFanu (1999) has observed that medicine now only recognizes one form of knowledge, that which "can be objectively and explicitly demonstrated with statistical techniques and clinical trails" (p. 362). In a blistering attack he observes:

> But, as has been observed repeatedly, the reverse is the case. It is this statistically derived knowledge that has consistently been shown to be unreliable, promoting the patently absurd as proven fact. Further, clinical trials cannot answer the sort of complex questions that frequently crop up in medical practice and when many are aggregated together, incomplete data is run through computer programs of bewildering complexity to produce results of implausible precision. (p. 362)

LeFanu (1999) notes that "this form of knowledge" has been shown to "result in the adoption of an ineffective treatment in 32 percent of cases and the rejection of a useful treatment in 33 percent of cases" (pp. 362–363). LeFanu (1999) observes that clinical field trials produced the right answer only a third of the time.

THE FOLLY OF CODIFYING CORRECT SCIENCE

While some rules may be necessary for the verification of discovery, true "scientific work" rarely proceeds along the lines of the so-called scientific method or its contemporary derivative in the NRC's (2002) "six guiding principles" (p. 52). True scientific work contains passion, imagination, artistry and represents a social construction rather than a discovery (Geison, 1995, p. 14). Even the greatest scientists such as Louis Pasteur did not follow the scientific method and engaged in practices that favored their own theories (Geison, 1995, p. 108; Judson, 2004, pp. 65–72). In defending Pasteur, Nobel Prize winning chemist Max Perutz (1995) also confessed that, "In fact, scientists rarely follow any of the scientific methods that philosophers have prescribed for them. They use their common sense" (p. 56).

What the NRC (2002) has done is to reformulate the rules for scientific research that is most likely going to reify known theories and their derivative practices. What these "guiding principles" as rules will most likely accomplish is to reify the idea of "correct science" that will result in true discoveries ("new eyes") being treated as heresies because they fail to follow the "rules." When they become embedded the protocols of grant review for government funding as they inevitably must, a rationale is built into the process which favors reinventing the known as opposed to probing the unknown and:

> Neither applicants nor panel members are likely to take risks. Unorthodox ideas, science that might turn out to be radically new, is not going to be funded through peer review. The point is plausible on its face and has been made repeatedly, vehemently, by eminent scientists . . . from their personal experience . . . the most perplexing variant of this that scientists raise is that the system favors safe research. (Judson, 2004, pp. 266–267)

The history of actual scientific discovery is as quirky and unpredictable as any enterprise in the human lexicon. Practicing scientists have long recognized its thoroughly subjective nature. In the words of Chien-Shiung Wu, an experimental nuclear physicist, "The main stumbling block in the way of any progress is and always has been unimpeachable tradition" (as cited in McGrayne, 1993, p. 279).

Robert Sternberg (2004) offered advice about embedding notions of good science in politics when he observed that "science has always proceeded best when it is left totally independent of the political process, and when competing schools of thought are left to slug it out on the scientific battlefield free of political influence or interference" (p. 56).

Rules for research that want sure things are unlikely to find any new ways to unlock the mysteries of human leadership in general and educational leadership in particular.

The inherently hidebound notion of science in the NRC's (2002) six guiding principles will likely ossify scientific discovery and work against any radical notion of change as Paul Feyerabend (1993) predicted:

> when scientists become accustomed to treating theories in a certain way, when they forget the reasons for this treatment but simply regard it as the "essence of science" or as an important part of what it means to be "scientific," when philosophers aid them in their forgetfulness by systematizing the familiar procedures and showing how they flow from an abstract theory of rationality then the theories needed to show the shortcomings of the underlying standards will not be introduced or, if they are introduced, will not

be taken seriously. They will not be taken seriously because they clash with customary habits and systemazations thereof. (p. 233)

The NRC's (2002) efforts to improve the quality of educational research and the institutionalization of correct science signals the triumph of processes of verification at the expense of discovery. The accepted theories of the day will dominate governmental funding. There is likely to be very little theory testing in the NRC's (2002) version of science. Churchland (1985) underscores the folly of this type of advocacy:

> Human reason is a hierarchy of heuristics for seeking, recognizing, storing and exploiting information. But those heuristics were invented at random, and they were selected for within a very narrow evolutionary environment, cosmologically speaking. It would be *miraculous* if human reason were completely free of false strategies and fundamental cognitive limitations, and doubly miraculous if the theories we accept failed to reflect those defects. (p. 36)

Finally, we ought to heed Maxwell's (2004) admonition of when he believes that randomized experiments would be merited in education and determine if these are applicable to a study of leadership and whether, if possible, they would produce anything we do not already know. Maxwell (2004) indicates that "strictly experimental designs" are merited only when (a) "a well-developed theory informs the intervention and research design and allows interpretation of the experimental results"; (b) the process being examined is "manipulable, fairly straightforward and simple . . . relatively free from temporal and contextual variability" that would only exist in "closed systems" (Sayer, 1992, pp. 121–125); and (c) "the situation is not open to direct investigation of causal processes" (Maxwell, 2004, p. 9). If educational administration can be so conceptualized then the NRC guidelines can be applied. Otherwise we need to look elsewhere for our models of research on leadership, even if it means eschewing governmental or foundational funding, and in going against popular antidotes derived from the world of business and supported by such agencies as the Broad Foundation or the Thomas B. Fordham Institute (see English, 2004b) or the Southern Regional Education Board (2004).

In commenting on why so many business books on leadership are so awful in an article entitled "How 51 Gorillas Can Make You Seriously Rich," *The Economist* (2004, August 21) observes:

Of course, the most perceptive leadership literature was written 400 years ago by William Shakespeare; and some of today's most readable books discuss the techniques of past heroes, such as Alexander the Great. They will teach you history, even if they do not make you Jack Welch. (p. 69)

What educational leadership research requires today are powerful, nuanced, contextually rich descriptions of leaders and collaborators (sometimes and erroneously called followers) conspiring and working in real schools with names, places, smells, and noises. What we need are morally imbued portraits of the complexity and interactions that comprise the drama of leadership (see Starratt, 1993), as opposed to the dreary depiction of generic patterns of nameless leaders in nameless schools who represent the summation of generic skills and dispositions embodied in the ISLLC standards and accreditation criteria (Hessel & Holloway, 2002). Above all, leadership is artistic performance. It is comprised of some skills no doubt, but it is an artful transcendence of content within context, symmetry in asymmetry, and clarity within ambiguity. When it comes to making any new discoveries about leadership, the NRC's six guiding principles aren't even wrong, for as Jacob Heilbrunn (1996) observed for the field of leadership studies ". . . to grow as a discipline, it will have to cast a wider net. Doing so, it may discover that the most important things about leadership lie far beyond the capabilities of science to analyze" (p. 11).

CONCLUSION

In conclusion, there are three major points which are important to consider in applying the NRC's guiding principles to a study of educational leadership. They are:

1. The NRC's criteria are a teleology, a doctrine that is considered true by design, but which offers no new promises for any discoveries in a study of leadership, and in fact, will lead to the reification of the role of an educational leader as an "orthodox-innovator," i.e., someone who sees the role of leader as carrying out the programs of the past (see Skowronek, 2002, p. 88). While it is true, as noted by Heck & Hallinger (1999) that, "Differences in how theoretical models of

school leadership are conceptualized and operationalized have important implications for the ways in which they are tested," the reverse is also true. To specify in advance like the NRC does that certain rules must be followed similarly advances certain models and methods as superior over others. In short, when the rules mandate only certain forms of examination, some models are much more amenable to such use than others. The view of leadership as advanced via the NRC's "six guiding principles" will reinforce traditional ideas of research in educational leadership, namely "the positivist pursuit of a structural interpretation of social processes" (Heck & Hallinger, 1999, p. 151).

2. The NRC's criteria are aimed mainly at studies involving verification of what is already known and actually contain an anti-change doctrine. The distinction between verification and discovery was advanced by Paul Feyerabend (1993) who articulated the difference between *the irrationality of discovery*, which may not follow any method or rules, and the *logic of justification*, which occurs after a discovery and which has to be rational in order to be accepted (p. 147). When it comes to the discovery process, Feyerabend (1993) summarized the meaning of this distinction as, "Without chaos no knowledge. Without a frequent dismissal of reason, no progress" (p. 158).

3. The NRC's stance obliterates leadership because real leadership in context is as much an art as a science. The "art" of leadership is highly situational and involves performance and drama where judgment regarding quality is centered on performance, as opposed to results obtained in the usual input-output model commonly used in school "effect" studies (Heck & Hallinger, 1999, pp. 144–145). Studies of leadership are not likely to be amenable to the criteria set forth by the NRC inasmuch as leaders are not the result of random processes, but are contextually and culturally specific, nor are "clinical trials" in the sense of leadership careers generalizable in the same way as replication in scientifically controlled experiments. To insist upon their application and reification will result in the closing-off of any possibilities of discovery, where by "discovery" is meant to "obtain sight of knowledge for the first time" (Merriam-Webster, 2003, p. 3570).

What is needed in the study of leadership are not new landscapes in the traditional sense of scientific "discovery," but rather having "new eyes" to focus on the old landscapes, i.e., a shift of perception. The critical distinction is that there are no new landscapes waiting to be "discovered," but only new mental constructs that will "see" what has always been there but which was invisible because the methods of discovery were the main impediment to developing "new eyes." Barash (2003) calls the creation of "new eyes" *retrocognition* whereby something is observed only after it is recognized within a new conceptual framework (p. B10). The NRC's six guiding principles work against the creation of such new conceptual frameworks by delegitimizing them because if they don't follow their rules they aren't "scientific."

REFERENCES

Ackerman, R., & Maslin-Ostrowski, P. (2002). *The wounded leader: How real leadership emerges in times of crisis.* San Francisco, CA: Jossey-Bass.

Aczel, A. (1999). *God's equation: Einstein, relativity, and the expanding universe.* New York: Four Walls Eight Windows.

Apple, M. (1982). *Education and power.* Boston: Routledge and Kegan Paul.

Barash, D. (2003, June 27). Believing is seeing. *The Chronicle of Higher Education*, pp. B10–11.

Beatty, B. (2000). The emotions of educational leadership: Breaking the silence. *International Journal of Leadership in Education, 3*(4), 331–357.

Begley, S. (2004, September 3). In physics, big errors can get the ball rolling toward big discoveries. *Wall Street Journal*, p. A7.

Bodanis, D. (2000). $E = mc^2$: *A biography of the world's most famous equation.* New York: Berkeley Publishing Company.

Burkhardt, H., & Schoenfeld, A. (2003, December). Improving educational research: Toward a more useful, more influential, and better-funded enterprise. *Educational Researcher, 32*(9), 3–14.

Caro, R. (2002). *The years of Lyndon Johnson: Master of the senate.* New York: Alfred Knopf.

Chandrasekhar, S. (1995, September 2). *The Economist*, p. 97.

Churchland, P. (1985). The ontological status of observables: In praise of the superempirical virtues. In P. Churchland & C. Hooker (Eds.), *Images of science: Essays on realism and empiricism* (pp. 35–47). Chicago: University of Chicago Press.

Conord, B., & Conord, J. (2002). *Costa Rica.* Edison, NJ: Hunter Publishing.

Conot, R. (1979). *A streak of luck: The life and legend of Thomas Alva Edison.* New York: Seaview Books.

Cook, T. (2002). Randomized experiments in educational policy research: A critical examination of the reasons the educational evaluation community has offered for not doing them. *Educational Evaluation and Policy Analysis, 24*(3), 175–199.

DeBono, E. (1972). *Po: Beyond yes and no.* New York: Penguin Books.

Dewey, J. (1929). *The sources of a science of education.* New York: Horace Liveright.

English, F. (2003). Cutter-cutter leaders for cookie cutter schools: The teleology of standardization and the de-legitimization of the university in educational leadership preparation. *Leadership and Policy in Schools, 2*(1), 27–46.

English, F. (2004a, Spring). Undoing the "done deal": Reductionism, ahistoricity, and pseudo-science in the knowledge base and standards for educational administration. *UCEA Review, 46,* 5–7.

English, F. (2004b). Learning "manifestospeak": A metadiscursive analysis of the Fordham Institute's and Broad Foundation's manifesto for better leaders for America's schools. In T. Lasley, II (Ed.), *Better leaders for America's schools: Perspectives on the manifesto.* Columbia, MO: UCEA, 52–91.

Fenwick, L. (2000). *The principal shortage: Who will lead?* Cambridge, MA: Harvard Graduate School of Education, The Principals Center & Spencer Foundation.

Feyerabend, P. (1993). *Against method.* London, UK: Verso.

Gadamer, H.-G. (1977). *Philosophical hermeneutics* (D.E. Linge, Trans.). Berkeley: University of California Press.

Gardner, H. (1995). *Leading minds: An anatomy of leadership.* New York: Harper Collins.

Geison, G. (1995). *The private science of Louis Pasteur.* Princeton, NJ: Princeton University Press.

Gilman, D., & Lanman-Givens, B. (2001). Where have all the principals gone? *Educational Leadership, 58*(8), 72–74.

Glass, T., Bjork, L., & Brunner, C. (2000). *The 2000 study of the American school superintendency.* Arlington, VA: American Association of School Administrators.

Gordon, C. (Ed.). (1980). *Power-knowledge: Selected interviews and other writings, 1972–1977 by Michel Foucault.* New York: Pantheon Books.

Gratzer, W. (2002). *Eurekas and euphorias: The Oxford book of scientific anecdotes.* Oxford, UK: Oxford University Press.

Greene, B. (2004). *The fabric of the cosmos: Space, time, and the texture of reality.* New York: Alfred A. Knopf.

Habermas, J. (1981). *The theory of communicative action: Vol. 1. Reason and the rationalization of society* (T. McCarthy, Trans.). Boston: Beacon Press.

Heck, R., & Hallinger, P. (1999). Next generation methods for the study of leadership and school improvement. In J. Murphy and K. Louis (Eds.), *Handbook of research on educational administration* (2nd ed., pp. 141–162). San Francisco, CA: Jossey-Bass.

Heilbrunn, J. (1996). Can leadership be studied? In P. Temes (Ed.), *Teaching leadership: Essays in theory and practice* (pp. 1–12). New York: Peter Lang.

Hessel, K., & Holloway, J. (2002). *A framework for school leaders: Linking the ISLLC standards to practice.* Princeton, NJ: ETS.

How 51 gorillas can make you seriously rich. (2004, August 21). *The Economist,* p. 69.

Johnson, P. (1996). Antipodes: Plato, Nietzsche, and the moral dimension of leadership. In P. Temes (Ed.), *Teaching leadership: Essays in theory and practice* (pp. 13–44). New York: Peter Lang.

Johnson, W., & Harper, G. (2005). *Becoming a leader the Annapolis way: 12 combat lessons from the navy's leadership academy.* New York: McGraw Hill.

Judson, H. (2004). *The great betrayal: Fraud in science.* Orlando, FL: Harcourt.

Katz, M. (1968). *The irony of early school reform.* Boston: Beacon Press.

Keegan, J. (1987). *The mask of command.* New York: Viking.

Klinker, J., & Hackmann, D. (2004). An analysis of principals' ethical decision making using Rest's four component model of moral behavior. *Journal of School Leadership, 14*(4), 434–456.

Kouzes, J., & Posner, B. (1987). *The leadership challenge.* San Francisco, CA: Jossey-Bass.

Kuhn, T. (1996). *The structure of scientific revolutions.* Chicago: University of Chicago Press.

Kupermintz, H. (2003). Teacher effects and teacher effectiveness: A validity investigation of the Tennessee value added assessment system. *Educational Evaluation and Policy Analysis, 25*(3), 287–298.

Lakatos, I. (1999). *The methodology of scientific research programmes.* Cambridge, UK: Cambridge University Press.

Lam, Y. (1984). Sources of managerial stress of the public school administrator: A typology. *Education, 10*(1), 48–52.

LeFanu, J. (1999). *The rise and fall of modern medicine.* New York: Carroll & Graf Publishers.

Levine, A. (2005). *Educating school leaders.* New York: Teachers College, Columbia, Schools of Education Research Project.

Lindle, J. (2004). Trauma and stress in the principal's office: Systematic inquiry as coping. *Journal of School Leadership, 14*(4), 378–410.

Maxwell, J. (2004, March). Causal explanation, qualitative research, and scientific inquiry in education. *Educational Researcher*, *33*(2), 3–11.

Mcg. Thomas, R. (1995, October 11). Gerald de Vaucouleurs, 77, galactic astronomer, is dead. *New York Times*, p. A12.

McGrayne, S. (1993). *Nobel prize winning women of science.* New York: Carol Publishing Group.

McLemee, S. (2004). Delving into democracy's shadows. *The Chronicle of Higher Education*, *51*(4), pp. A10–A14.

Merriam-Webster. (2003). *Merriam-Webster's collegiate dictionary* (11th ed.). Springfield, MA: Merriam-Webster.

National Research Council (NRC) Committee Scientific Principles for Education Research (2002). *Scientific research in education.* R. J. Shavelson & L. Towne (Eds.). Washington, DC: National Academy Press.

Oakes, J. (1985). *Keeping track: How schools structure inequality.* New Haven, CT: Yale University Press.

Patterson, J. (2000). *The anguish of leadership.* Arlington, VA: American Association of School Administrators.

Perutz, M. (1995, December 21). The pioneer defended. *New York Review of Books*, *42*(20), 54–58.

Phillips, D., & Loy, J. (2003). *Character in action: The U.S. Coast Guard on leadership.* Annapolis, MD: Naval Institute Press.

Regalado, A. (2005, February 14). In climate debate, the "hockey stick" leads to a face-off. *Wall Street Journal*, pp. A1, A13.

Riehl, C., Larson, C., Short, P., & Reitzug, U. (2000). Research and scholarship in educational administration: Learning to know, knowing to do, doing to learn. *Educational Administration Quarterly*, *36* (3), 391–427.

Sanders, W. (1988). Value-added assessment. *The School Administrator*, *55*, 11.

Sanders, W., & Horn, P. (1994). The Tennessee Valued-Added Assessment System (TVASS): Mixed-model methodology in educational assessment. *Journal of Personnel Evaluation in Education*, *8*, 299–311.

Sapon-Shevin, M. (1994). *Playing favorites: Gifted education and the disruption of community.* Albany: State University of New York Press.

Sarason, S. (1990). *The predictable failure of educational reform.* San Francisco, CA: Jossey-Bass.

Sayer, A. (1992). *Method in social science: A realist approach* (2nd ed.). London: Routledge.

Skowronek, S. (2002). *The politics presidents make: Leadership from John Adams to Bill Clinton.* Cambridge, MA: Harvard University Press.

Southern Regional Education Board. (2004). *Progress being made in getting a quality leader in every school.* Atlanta, GA: Author.

Spring, J. (1976). *The sorting machine.* New York: Longman.

Spring, J. (1989). *The sorting machine revisited: National educational policy since 1945* (updated edition). New York: Longman.

Starratt, R. (1993). *The drama of leadership.* London: Falmer Press.

St. Pierre, E. (2002, November). "Science" rejects postmodernism. *Educational Researcher, 31*(8), 25–27.

Sternberg, R. (2004, October 27). Good intentions, bad results: A dozen reasons why the no child left behind act is failing our schools. *Education Week, 24*(9), 56.

Thomas, G. (1997). What's the use of theory? *Harvard Educational Review, 67*(1), 75–104.

Valelly, R. (2003, October 31). An overlooked theory on presidential politics. *Chronicle of Higher Education,* pp. B10–12.

2

Scientific Research in Education: Implications for Culturally Sensitive Research Frameworks in Educational Leadership

Linda C. Tillman, University of North Carolina at Chapel Hill

Since the publication of *Scientific Research in Education* (2002), a report of the National Research Council (NRC), there have been numerous responses and critiques with respect to the advantages and disadvantages of the definition and guidelines for "scientific research" in education.[1] In a recent special issue of *Teachers College Record*, Margaret Eisenhart (2005), a member of the NRC committee, noted:

> As a consensus report created by 16 researchers and a study director, sponsored by several agencies, written in a year's time in an effort to influence congressional legislation, and potentially affecting the lives of thousands of researchers and hundreds of thousands of students and teachers, the production of SRE [scientific research in education] is situated not in one theory but multiple theories. It is also situated in politics, group dynamics, history, and context. To say it is a compromise(d) document is an understatement; to say it is not perfect is correct; to say it is was not well-intentioned is inappropriate. (p. 52)

Eisenhart's comments speak to the complex issues embedded in a report that has added fuel to debates about what constitutes research and how various types of research can contribute to a socially just and equitable educational system that benefits *all* children. Of particular importance to the discussions about what constitutes research is the report's distinction between scientific research and educational research. While it is not within the scope of this chapter to enter into a lengthy discussion about the rationale and consequences of this distinction, it is worth noting that such a distinction sets up an "us" and "them" dichotomy where *educational researchers* appear to assume a status that is less important in the larger research community. The NRC's argument that research that does not lend itself to controlled conditions raises the question of whose research is valued, privileged and acknowledged by those who control the funding and the dissemination of research.

It should be acknowledged that a primary purpose of the NRC report is to articulate the importance of educational research to educational policymakers and congressional representatives who make decisions about who will receive funding and what kinds of research will be funded. Thus, to a great extent the NRC committee responded to impending structural changes at the federal level. At the same time, the report left open the possibility that thousands of educational researchers who do not conduct experimental research would likely find it difficult to obtain funding for projects that could potentially have a significant impact on the field of education.

The purpose of this chapter is to explore the utility of the NRC's principles of scientific research in light of the increased use of racially and culturally sensitive research approaches in educational research. Specifically, I make a hypothetical assumption that all educational research is conducted based on the NRC principles. Given this hypothetical assumption, I discuss in what ways the principles are consistent or inconsistent with the criteria of Tillman's (2002) Culturally Sensitive Research Framework (CSRF). Using educational leadership as the field of inquiry, I provide examples of research on African Americans in school leadership that employ components of the CSRF and discuss to what extent the NRC principles are supported in the research. I conclude the discussion with implications for research practice in the field of educational leadership.

CULTURALLY SENSITIVE RESEARCH APPROACHES: A NECESSARY PARADIGM SHIFT

Siddle Walker (2005) was one of the many prominent scholars who responded to the NRC report. She noted that in her historical and ethnographic work on Blacks in segregated schools in the South, her ethnic affiliation with the community "assisted in the research process in important ways that were not taught in my graduate methods classes" (p. 31). For Siddle Walker as well other African American researchers, same-race and cultural affiliation, access to African American participants, knowledge of African American cultural norms and data interpretations based on co-constructed narratives are fundamental to the research inquiry in African American communities. Yet, the NRC committee clearly makes a distinction between scientific research and other forms of research that are "less scientific" such as that conducted by Siddle Walker. The authors of the report cite the work of Eisner (1991), Lawrence-Lightfoot (1994), and Lawrence-Lightfoot and Davis (1997) as "examples to illustrate the distinguishing character of our principles of science" (p. 74). The discussion of connoisseurship and portraiture appears to minimize this genre of research as having limited credibility in the larger research community and marginalizes its value. The NRC critique of this work also suggests that these methods of inquiry fall into some other obscure category of research outside the domain of more important "scientific" research.

Increasingly it is the case that African Americans and other scholars of color conduct insider research in their own communities. This research is supported by a growing body of scholarship focused on conducting research under the umbrella term "people of color" (for example, Banks, 1998; Delgado Bernal, 1998; Stanfield, 1994; Tillman, 2002, 2005, 2006), and the use of qualitative research approaches that place the *culture* of an ethnic group at the center of the inquiry. Stanfield (1994) argued for the creation of qualitative research methods that are indigenous to African Americans and other people of color. According to Stanfield, the key features of an indigenous paradigm are the creation of a family of qualitative research paradigms, derived theories, methodologies, and styles of interpretations that more adequately reflect the plurality of American society and the global community. Stanfield further argued that conventional literature on race (particularly in qualitative research) suffers from the absence of a conceptual framework for understanding how dominant structures organize, marginalize and even exclude knowledge production regarding African Americans.

Tillman's (2002) Culturally Sensitive Research Framework is an alternative to dominant quantitative and qualitative research paradigms. A theoretical framework for culturally sensitive research approaches for African Americans is based on culturally congruent research methods, culturally specific knowledge, cultural resistance to theoretical dominance, culturally sensitive data interpretations, and culturally informed theory and practice. Individually and collectively these principles are representative of epistemological and methodological possibilities for more culturally informed research, theory, and practice.

Culturally Congruent Research Methods

Culturally sensitive research approaches use qualitative methods such as interviews (individual, group, life history) observation, and participant-observation. These and other qualitative methods are used to investigate and capture a holistic contextualized picture of the social, political, economic, and educational factors that affect the everyday existence of African Americans, particularly in educational settings.

Culturally Specific Knowledge

Culturally sensitive research approaches use the particular and unique self-defined (Black self-representation) experiences of African Americans. The researcher is committed to and accepts the responsibility for maintaining the cultural integrity of the participants and other members of the community. Researchers carefully consider the extent of their own cultural knowledge, cross-race and same-race perspectives, and insider/ outsider issues related to the research process.

Cultural Resistance to Theoretical Dominance

Culturally sensitive research approaches attempt to reveal, understand, and respond to unequal power relations that may minimize, marginalize, subjugate or exclude the multiple realities and knowledge bases of African Americans. Research privilege is questioned, as well as claims of neutrality and objectivity in educational research. Research practices that place the perspectives of African Americans on the margins of the inquiry are challenged. The cultural standpoints of those persons who experience the social, political, economic, and educational consequences of unequal power relations are privileged over the assumed knowledge of those who are positioned outside of these experiences.

Culturally Sensitive Data Interpretations

Culturally sensitive research approaches for African Americans position experiential knowledge as legitimate, appropriate, and necessary for analyzing, understanding, and reporting data. Analysis and presentation that is appropriate to the research topic and the individual or group under study is co-constructed. Storytelling, family histories, biographies, narratives as well as other forms of data presentation may be used. The cultural standpoints of African Americans provide "endarkened" analyses of their particular experiences in American society.

Culturally Informed Theory and Practice

Culturally sensitive research approaches can lead to the development of theories and practices that are intended to address the culturally specific circumstances of the lives of African Americans. Researchers rely on participants' perspectives and cultural understandings of the phenomena under study to establish connections between espoused theory and reality, and then to generate theory based on these "endarkened" perspectives. Researchers use culturally informed knowledge to propose educational change, and work to build meaningful, productive relationships with the non-academic community.

Culturally based research frameworks do not include the complete range of possibilities for conducting research in African American and other communities of color. However, the Culturally Sensitive Research Framework places African Americans at the center, rather than on the margin of the inquiry and allows researchers to situate themselves based on their own cultural knowledge.

SCIENTIFIC AND CULTURALLY SENSITIVE RESEARCH APPROACHES IN EDUCATIONAL LEADERSHIP

According to the National Research Council report, the following six guiding principles underlie all scientific inquiry, including educational research: (a) Pose significant questions that can be investigated empirically, (b) link research to relevant theory, (c) use methods that permit direct investigation of the question, (d) provide a coherent and explicit chain of reasoning, (e) replicate and generalize across studies, and (f) disclose research to encourage professional scrutiny and critique. In the next section, I discuss to what extent the NRC principles are consistent with the criteria of the Culturally Sensitive Research Framework. I also discuss several studies on African Americans in school leadership that incorporate components of the CSRF.

Scientific Principle 1: Pose Significant
Questions That Can Be Investigated Empirically

Scientific principle 1 posits that researchers will (a) [pose] significant questions about the world with potentially multiple answers that lead to hypotheses or conjectures that can be tested or refuted, and (b) [questions] would be posed in such a way that it is possible to test the adequacy of alternative answers through carefully designed and implemented observations (NRC, 2002, pp. 54–55). A major purpose of the Culturally Sensitive Research Framework is to provide researchers opportunities to pose questions that are important to the leadership and participation of African Americans in education and U.S. society. Investigations of phenomena that are specific to African Americans are intended to capture the range of their experiences in educational contexts, such as educational leadership. The CSRF criteria are not intended to support the articulation of hypothesis that can be *tested*. Rather, the CSRF provides opportunities for researchers to design and conduct observations of individuals in a variety of settings and to confirm the existence of similar circumstances for African Americans in multiple contexts.

The use of components of the CSRF such as *culturally sensitive research methods* (for example, interviews and observations) provide researchers opportunities to not only pose culturally significant questions but also provides opportunities for participants to make decisions about the cultural significance of the questions given their particular circumstances. Culturally sensitive research approaches attempt to capture the *culturally specific knowledge* (the unique self-defined experiences of African Americans) generate new knowledge, contribute to existing knowledge bases, and fill theoretical gaps with respect to the lived experiences of African Americans. While the NRC principles of inquiry appear to define empirically based knowledge as only that knowledge which results from the use of quantitative methods, culturally sensitive qualitative methods are useful in uncovering the range of beliefs, attitudes, and theories articulated by African Americans—knowledge that may be more difficult to uncover using methods that rely on tests or measurements.

The emphasis of NRC principle 1 on the significance of the research question raises two points: for whom are the research questions significant, and who has the authority to decide whether the questions are significant? Indeed research questions about African Americans in school leadership are not only important to African Americans but are also important to the field of educational leadership. Tillman (2006) conducted a study of the role of African American principals in facilitating the personal and professional competence of novice teachers in an urban school district. She found that collectively the principals believed all novice teachers can benefit from mentoring and that principals must take active rather than passive roles in facilitating effective mentoring. The research questions were important to the principals who participated in her study. However, the principals chose to raise other questions they believed were also equally, if not more important than the narrowly defined topic of mentoring. Thus, they also discussed the predominantly African American urban school context and the extent to which the complexities of the urban context affected teaching and learning, as well as their capacity to lead. Drawing on their experiential knowledge and their racial and cultural insider status, they talked about the condition of urban education for African American students, the need for qualified and committed teachers, the imperative of working with African American parents, and internal and external factors that affect African American student achievement. Thus, the concept of *principal as mentor* took on a different dimension for these principals. More than mentoring new teachers about tasks typically identified in the literature (which include emotional, physical, instructional and institutional support), these principals believed that mentoring teachers was one way to convey their commitment to not only facilitating teacher competency, but to the academic success of African American students. According to the principals, conveying this commitment is particularly important in the African American urban school context since the teaching force remains predominantly White, and cross-race student-teacher interactions can be a critical factor in promoting student self-esteem and student success.

Tillman's research addresses a gap in the existing knowledge base with respect to the leadership of African American principals as well as the concept of principal as mentor. Like teacher education, the field of educational leadership is predominantly White, both in the professorate and practitioner ranks. Thus, research questions (and their significance) that lead too much of the theory and practice of educational leadership is typically presented from the perspective of Whites and particularly White males.[2] The question of *who* determines the significance of the research question is one that must be considered when conducting research on African American school leaders. The absence of culturally informed perspectives and co-construction of the knowledge base as suggested by NRC principle 1 can further marginalize the research, theory and practice of African Americans in educational leadership. By employing *cultural resistance to theoretical dominance* "the cultural standpoints of those persons who experience the social, political, economic, and educational consequences of unequal power relations are privileged over the assumed knowledge of those who are positioned outside of these experiences" (Tillman, 2002, p. 6).

NRC principle 1 is consistent with the purposes and criteria of the CSRF with respect to posing significant questions about phenomena that affect African Americans in school leadership. Indeed there are multiple contexts, stories, and explanations that should be investigated to identify specific factors that affect the leadership capacity of African Americans in preK–12 schooling. However, the NRC requirements for hypotheses generation and testing are inconsistent with the purposes of the CSRF and have the potential to contribute to a narrow view of African Americans in school leadership.

Scientific Principle 2: Link Research to Relevant Theory

Scientific principle 2 posits that theory connects to the research process by (a) [the use of a] conceptual framework, model or theory that suggests possible questions to ask or answers to the question posed, and (b) all scientific observations are "theory laden" (NRC, 2002, pp. 61–62). With the exception of the emphasis on "scientific observation," NRC principle 2 is consistent with the criteria and purposes of the CSRF. The CSRF is itself a theoretical framework for conducting research and generating theory about African Americans in education and U.S. society. Individually and collectively the components of the framework are representative of epistemological and methodological possibilities for more culturally informed research, theory, and practice. The components of the framework also provide opportunities for researchers to apply other conceptual frameworks, models and theories. Importantly, it also provides opportunities for participants to engage in theory generation. Thus, there is no assumption that the researcher has the right to *impose* theory on the participants.

Lomotey (1993) used components of the CSRF in case studies of African American female elementary principals who were responsible for implementing an African and African American curriculum infusion project. Lomotey conducted in-depth interviews and observations (*culturally congruent research methods*) to gain the principals' perspectives about the innovative curriculum project. Principals talked about the importance of the new curriculum for African American students, the importance of helping teachers to understand the subject matter content, and helping teachers to understand the need for this particular curriculum. Moving beyond the topic of the curriculum initiative, the principals used their *culturally specific knowledge* to convey how they worked with African American students, how they worked with students' families and communities, and how they promoted self-esteem and educational excellence for all students. Based on the findings, Lomotey developed a conceptual framework for African American principal leadership. Four components of principal leadership make up the *bureaucrat/administrator* role identity: the ability to (a) develop goals, (b) harness the energy of the staff, (c) facilitate communication, and (d) be involved in instructional management. The qualities of commitment, confidence, and compassion make up the *ethno-humanist* role identity. According to Lomotey, the primary goal of a principal who assumes a bureaucrat/administrator role identity is "schooling"—facilitating the movement of students from grade to grade. The primary goal of a principal who assumes an ethno-humanist role identity is "education"—meeting a set of cultural goals.

Lomotey's bureaucrat/administrator and ethno-humanist framework represents a particular theory and has been used in studies investigating the leadership behaviors and styles of African American principals.[3] The theory has been used to analyze, explain, understand, and build on the theory and practice of principal leadership from an African American perspective and has led to *culturally informed theory and practice* about African Americans in the principalship. Lomotey's theory is not intended to test a hypothesis about principal leadership generally. It draws on the *culturally specific knowledge* of African American principals and employs *cultural resistance to theoretical dominance* rather than relying on dominant theories. Researchers who use the theory rely on the participants' cultural understanding of school leadership to generate new theory, to make connections between theory and practice, and to promote educational change.

Because the leadership of African Americans as a specific field of study is underdeveloped in the traditional educational leadership literature, theories related to leaders' same-race and cultural affiliation, leadership styles, recruitment, hiring and retention of African American leaders, instructional supervision, leadership in urban schools, and the relationship between African American school leadership and African American student success are yet to be fully articulated. Thus, like Siddle Walker (2005) who found a limited and undeveloped theoretical base for investigating and understanding the leadership and participation of African American principals in the segregated schooling of the South, there is a wealth of undocumented theory about the leadership of African Americans in public and private schools. For example, Tillman (2005) found that while the majority of African American principals work in urban schools, no specific lines of research or theories on African Americans in the principalship are evident in the general category of urban school leadership. The CSRF increases the possibilities for developing lines of research on African Americans in school leadership that draw on their culturally informed knowledge in various school contexts.

Scientific Principle 3: Use Methods That
Permit Direct Investigation of the Question

Scientific principle 3 posits that (1) research methods—the design for collecting data and the measurement and analysis of variables in the design—should be selected in light of the research question, and should directly address it, and (2) the link between question and method must be clearly explicated and justified (NRC, 2002, pp. 61–62). Principle 3 emphasizes research methods; that is, how the data will be collected and analyzed based on the major research question for study. Principle 3 also suggests that the question must fit the method and the researcher is responsible for fully implementing the method. Emphasis is also placed on measurement as a "key aspect of the research method" (p. 66). While it is acknowledged that culturally sensitive research can apply to studies using quantitative methods (Tillman, 2002), the CSRF does not seek to *measure* the experiences of African Americans in educational contexts such as school leadership. The requirement to measure (or reduce) an individual's perspective to a percentage or some other numerical category typically implies a Black-White racial comparison[4] and is contradictory to the major purpose of the framework—the investigation of a phenomenon from a specific position of color.

NRC principle 3 is consistent with two components of the CSRF: *culturally congruent research methods* and *culturally sensitive data interpretations*. Qualitative methods such as interviews (individual, group, life history), observations and participant observations have been used by researchers to investigate and capture holistic, contextualized pictures of factors that affect African Americans in educational settings. For example, Siddle Walker (2003) conducted extensive in-depth interviews with an African American principal in the South in an effort to contribute to the scholarship on African American principals in the pre- and post-*Brown* eras that would "expand the narrow lens through which Black leadership has historically been viewed" (p. 59). Similarly, Bloom and Erlandson (2003) used in-depth interviews to document the perspectives of African American female principals in urban schools and to add to the paucity of literature on African American female leaders in traditional educational leadership/administration journals.[5]

In the studies noted, researchers used *culturally sensitive data interpretations* to present the research from the self-defined perspective of African American principals. Using a particular theory (for example, feminist, standpoint, ethno-humanist, interpersonal caring) to guide the research inquiry, the researchers placed the knowledge of the participants at the center of the inquiry rather than on the margins. The researchers also presented co-constructed narratives in the form of life histories, biographies, and case studies. The interpretations drew on the cultural standpoints and the particular experiences of African American principals in particular circumstances. Given the oral tradition of African Americans (Stanfield, 1994), the research methods and data interpretations were consistent with NRC principle 3 and serve to contribute to the multiple standpoints that represent the whole of educational research.

Scientific Principle 4: Provide a Coherent, Explicit Chain of Reasoning

Scientific principle 4 posits the development of a logical chain of reasoning that is coherent and persuasive. The CSRF emphasizes rigorous research, but unlike principle 4 the framework does not emphasize hypotheses testing using if-then rules and inferences. Rather the components of the framework are intended to allow the researcher and the participants to tell a story that makes sense (is persuasive) and is consistent (logical) with their experiences—experiences that for African Americans are often difficult to reduce to an "if this, then that" analysis. Additionally, the issue of selection bias as articulated in principle 4 is inconsistent with the CSRF framework. Consistent with the genre of qualitative research, African American participants are likely to be selected based on community nomination (Foster, 1997) or other forms of purposeful sampling. One of the purposes of this intentional selection is to identify participants who have *culturally specific knowledge*, rather than general knowledge, about a particular phenomenon. For example, Reitzug and Patterson (1998) conducted a study of a Black female middle school principal in an urban school district. According to Reitzug and Patterson, the principal was selected for the study because of her reputation as an outstanding leader. Her community nomination came from several principals, and her reputation was verified by teachers as well as other educators. The purposeful selection of participants who have direct experience with respect to a particular phenomenon (such as the leadership roles of African American principals in urban districts) is intended to address issues related to credibility of the data.

When conducting research on African American leaders, it may be difficult to apply "rigorous reasoning" to racism, inequitable funding, tracking, disparities in school types (urban vs. rural vs. suburban), hiring practices and other factors that affect the leadership capacity of African Americans. Thus, given the NRC guideline to provide a coherent, explicit chain of reasoning, the perspectives of African Americans might well be silenced or viewed as suspect. As Stanfield (1994) argued, "no matter how people of color define themselves, there are still the more dominant stereotypes embedded in public culture that define their status and identities in the cosmos of the dominant" (p. 182). In addition, Tate (1994) has cautioned that no amount of experience or expertise will validate the scholarship of African American scholars who focus on the issue of race:

rather, it will only be viewed as "special pleading" (p. 264). In her response to the NRC report, Siddle Walker (2005) noted that even when African American researchers employ rigorous methods and apply a coherent, explicit chain of reasoning, rarely are their perspectives included in national debates on school reform. According to Siddle Walker,

> Consider the research on effective teaching behaviors that support African American student success. For over a decade, this knowledge base has been systematically built by researchers such as Jackie Irvine, Gloria Ladson-Billings, Michele Foster and others; it now demonstrates the school and community values, both historically and contemporarily, that appear to undergird an African American teaching epistemology. However, neither within nor without the scholarly community are their findings incorporated into the larger scholarly debate on school reform. Like the Black scholars of the previous century, it is as though they are heard only within their community. (p. 35)

To some extent, the requirements of NRC principle 4 support the existing culture of educational leadership—the absence of a distinct line of scholarship that focuses on the voices and perspectives of African American scholars and practitioners.[6] Adherence to the requirements of the principle in an absolute sense would further marginalize the research, scholarship, and theory of African Americans as well as other scholars who conduct research on African American school leadership.

Scientific Principle 5: Replicate and Generalize Across Studies

Scientific principle 5 posits that "replication and generalization strengthen and clarify the limits of scientific conjectures and theories" (NRC, 2002, p. 70). Principle 5 is consistent with the CSRF with respect to replicating studies to clarify and strengthen theories. Thus, it is expected that researchers who use components of the CSRF will conduct research that can be replicated by other researchers. This is especially important in research on African Americans in educational contexts, since as has been noted earlier their perspectives and experiences continue to be either excluded, placed on the margins, or presented using deficit frameworks and theories. For example, Tillman (2005) found that there is a paucity of literature in traditional educational leadership journals that documents the history and contributions of African American principals. Rather, the history of educational leadership focuses primarily on the contributions and theories of White males (see, for example, Leithwood and Duke, 1999). This emphasis presents a somewhat one-sided view of educational leadership and ignores the contributions of African Americans who built schools and served as principals and headmasters as early as 1865 (Anderson, 1988).

Principle 5 is inconsistent with the purposes and criteria of the CSRF with respect to the requirement to generalize findings. Consistent with the fundamentals of qualitative research, it is not the intent of the CSRF to generalize results to broader populations. Rather, like the majority of all qualitative research, the framework is intended to allow researchers to uncover particular circumstances of a particular individual or group at a particular time in a particular place. Generalization may be particularly problematic with respect to research on African Americans in educational leadership. For example, while the number of African Americans in the principalship is increasing, the field continues to be predominantly White. Moreover, the educational leadership professorate is also dominated by White males. Thus there are a limited number of African Americans who investigate issues affecting African American school leaders. Issues of reliability and validity as articulated in NRC principle 5 are also inconsistent with the CSRF. Rather there is an emphasis in the framework on trustworthiness and the *culturally specific knowledge* of the participants. In addition, the framework places emphasis on maintaining the cultural integrity of the participants, and researchers "carefully consider the extent of their own cultural knowledge, cross-race and same-race perspectives, and insider and outsider issues related to the research process" (Tillman, 2002, p. 6).

Scientific Principle 6: Disclose Research
to Encourage Professional Scrutiny and Critique

Scientific principle 6 posits that "regardless of the medium, the goals of research reporting are to communicate the findings from the investigation; to open the study to examination, criticism, review, and replication by peer investigators; and ultimately to incorporate the new knowledge into the prevailing canon of the field" (NRC, 2002, p. 72). Emphasis is placed on making the research public and "[allowing] the community of scientists and analysts to comprehend, to replicate and otherwise inform theory, research, and practice in that area" (p. 73). Principle 6 is consistent with the purposes of the CSRF. There is a need to conduct research on African Americans in school leadership that will be reviewed, discussed, and replicated by the larger educational leadership research community. Such critique can lead to *culturally informed theory and practice*. There is also a need for research on African Americans in school leadership that connects theory and reality and which leads to educational change that is socially just and benefits *all* students. To a great extent, principle 6 embodies the purposes of all educational research—to inform theory, research, and practice in all aspects of education.

CONCLUSION

The National Research Council's scientific principles can be viewed from a variety of theoretical, epistemological and methodological perspectives. Some scholars will readily agree with the principles, while other scholars may disregard the principles. I have taken the position in this chapter that the NRC principles can be useful from two standpoints: (1) The principles provide researchers with a framework that can be useful in deciding what is and is not important in the conceptualization, design, collection and analysis of specific types of research, and (2) the principles may provide a template for those researchers whose research depends on tests, measurements, and inferences. However, I also believe that the strict definition of "scientific research" is troublesome and strict adherence to the NRC principles of inquiry overlooks racially and culturally sensitive research frameworks such as the Culturally Sensitive Research Framework.

When considering the NRC principles individually, principles 2, 4, and 6 are most closely aligned with the criteria and purposes of the CSRF. However, as a whole the principles marginalize researchers who do not use quantitative methods. Importantly, a requirement to use the principles can impede research on significant topics such as school reform, the education of special populations, and the achievement gap as these issues relate to African Americans. Given the rapidly changing demographics of U.S. schooling and society, it is imperative that researchers consider the utility of culturally sensitive research when conducting research in racially and ethnically diverse schools and communities. I have used the phrase "The CSRF provides opportunities for researchers to . . ." several times in this chapter. My use of this wording is intentional as I believe it is imperative that all researchers be given opportunities to pose significant questions, design research, and collect, analyze and report findings that are important to the specific social, emotional and academic circumstances of African Americans and other people of color. In an extensive review of the literature of African Americans in the principalship (Tillman, 2004), I found a lack of research on African Americans in school leadership reported in educational leadership/administration journals. The somewhat exclusionary nature of the NRC guidelines would likely mean a continuation of the marginalization of research on African Americans in school leadership. As professionals, if our goals and objectives include working toward an educational system that is equitable and socially just, we must move beyond narrow and restrictive definitions and guidelines of "scientific" research to research paradigms that are more inclusive and reflective of our society. In addition, culturally sensitive research frameworks can produce findings that can be useful to African American and other leaders of color who are faced with the complex task of leading in diverse school contexts.

NOTES

1. For example see special issues of *Qualitative Inquiry, 10*(1) and *10*(2) (Cannella & Lincoln, 2004; Lincoln & Cannella, 2004) and *Teachers College Record, 107*(1) (Lather & Moss, 2005).

2. Much of the literature on school leadership that has shaped the field has been written by Whites. For example, see Boyan (1988), Murphy & Seashore Louis (1999) and Hallinger & Heck (1996).

3. For example see Gooden (2005), Bryant, (1998) and Loder (2005) for examples of studies that draw on Lomotey's bureaucrat-administrator and ethnohumanist framework.

4. Graham (1992) in a discussion of research in journals of the American Psychological Association notes that African Americans are usually compared to Whites in empirical studies (particularly in studies of intelligence and personality) and that White researchers often assign social class designations based on their own subjective impressions about the communities from which African American participants are drawn. In addition, in studies where African Americans

are compared to Whites, the race of the researcher and the socioeconomic status of the subjects can seriously confound the findings because these factors are rarely incorporated into the research designs. According to Graham (2002), "In contemporary society, most of the population is not White and middle class. Neither should the subject populations in the journals of our discipline be so disproportionate (p. 638).

5. For other examples of the use of culturally congruent research methods see Reitzug and Patterson (1998), Dillard (1995), and Mertz and McNeely (1998) who used interviews and observations in their studies of African American principals.

6. Benham (1997) notes that the absence of studies of African American women are, to a great degree "an educational leadership discourse and practice that has been structured to impede such treatment" (p. 282). Additionally, Bloom and Erlandson (2003) note "Findings from a minority insider's perspective are regarded as dubious and unlikely to be published in professional journals. Suspect conclusions are summarily ignored or dismissed, seldom becoming a part of administrative leadership theory" (p. 344).

REFERENCES

Anderson, J. D. (1988). *The education of blacks in the south, 1860–1935.* Chapel Hill: University of North Carolina Press.

Banks, J. (1998). The lives and values of researchers: Implications for educating citizens in a multicultural society. *Educational Researcher, 27*(2), 4–17.

Benham, M. K. P. (1997). Silences and serenades: The journeys of three ethnic minority women school leaders. *Anthropology and Education Quarterly, 28*(2), 280–307.

Bloom, C. M., & Erlandson, D. A. (2003). African American women principals in urban schools: Realities, (re)constructions, and resolutions. *Educational Administration Quarterly, 39*(3), 339–369.

Boyan, N. (Ed.). (1988). *Handbook of research on educational administration: A project of the American Educational Research Association.* New York: Longmans.

Bryant, N. (1998). Reducing the relational distance between actors: A case study in school reform. *Urban Education, 33*(1), 34–49.

Cannella, G. S., & Lincoln, Y. S. (Eds.). (2004). Dangerous discourses II: Comprehending and countering the redeployment of discourses (and resources) in the generation of liberatory inquiry. Special issue of *Qualitative Inquiry, 10*(2).

Delgado Bernal, D. (1998). Using a Chicana feminist epistemology in educational research. *Harvard Educational Review, 68*(4), 555–582.

Dillard, C. (1995). Leading with her life: An African American feminist (re)interpretation of leadership for an urban high school principal. *Educational Administration Quarterly, 31*(4), 539–563.

Eisenhart, M. (2005). Science plus: A response to the responses to *Scientific Research in Education. Teachers College Record, 107*(1), 52–58.

Eisner, E. (1991). *The enlightened eye: Qualitative inquiry and the enhancement of educational practice.* New York: Macmillan.

Foster, M. (1997). *Black teachers on teaching.* New York: New Press.

Gooden, M. A. (2005). The role of an African American principal in an urban information technology high school. *Educational Administration Quarterly, 41*(4), 630–650.

Graham, S. (1992). Most of the subjects were White and middle class: Trends in published research on African Americans in selected APA journals, 1970–1989. *American Psychologist, 47*(5), 629–639.

Hallinger, P., & Heck, R. H. (1996). Reassessing the principal's role in school effectiveness: A review of empirical research, 1980–1995. *Educational Administration Quarterly, 32*(1), 5–44.

Lather, P., & Moss, P. A. (Eds.). (2005, January). A symposium on the implications of the *Scientific Research in Education* report for qualitative inquiry. Special issue of *Teachers College Record, 107*(1).

Lawrence-Lightfoot, S. (1994). *I've known rivers: Lives of loss and liberation.* Reading, MA: Addison-Wesley.

Lawrence-Lightfoot, S., & Davis, J. H. (1997). *The art and science of portraiture.* San Francisco, CA: Jossey-Bass.

Leithwood, K., & Duke, L. (1999). A century's quest to understand school leadership. In J. Murphy & K. Seashore Louis (Eds.), *The handbook of research on educational administration* (2nd ed., pp. 45–72). San Francisco, CA: Jossey-Bass.

Lincoln, Y. S., & Cannella, G. S. (Eds.) (2004). Dangerous discourses: Methodological conservatism and governmental regimes of truth. Special issue of *Qualitative Inquiry, 10*(1).

Loder, T. L. (2005). African American women principals' reflections on social change, community othermothering, and Chicago public school reform. *Urban Education, 40*(3), 298–320.

Lomotey, K. (1993). African-American principals: Bureaucrat/administrators and Ethno-humanists. *Urban Education, 27*(4), 394–412.

Mertz, N. T., & McNeely, S. R. (1998). Women on the job: A study of female high school principals. *Educational Administration Quarterly, 34*(2), 196–222.

Murphy, J., & Seashore Louis, K. (Eds.) (1999). *Handbook of research on educational administration: A project of the American Educational Research Association* (2nd ed.). San Francisco, CA: Jossey-Bass.

National Research Council (NRC) Committee on Scientific Principles in Education Research. (2002). *Scientific research in education.* R. J. Shavelson & L. Towne (Eds.).Washington, DC: National Academic Press.

Reitzug, U. C., & Patterson, J. (1998). "I'm not going to lose you!" Empowerment through caring in an urban principal's practice with students. *Urban Education, 33*(2), 150–181.

Siddle Walker, V. (2003). The architects of Black schooling in the segregated south: The case of one principal leader. *Journal of Curriculum and Supervision, 19*(1), 54–72.

Siddle Walker, V. (2005). After methods, then what? A researcher's response to the report of the National Research Council. *Teachers College Record, 107*(1), 30–37.

Stanfield, J. (1994). Ethnic modeling in qualitative research. In N. Denzin & Y. Lincoln (Eds.), *Handbook of qualitative research* (pp. 176–188). Newbury Park, CA: Sage Publications.

Tate, W. (1994). From inner city to ivory tower: Does my voice matter in the academy? *Urban Education, 29*(3), 245–269.

Tillman, L. C. (2002). Culturally sensitive research approaches: An African American perspective. *Educational Researcher, 31*(9), 3–12.

Tillman, L. C. (2004). African American principals and the legacy of *Brown. Review of Research in Education, 28,* 101–146.

Tillman, L. C. (2005). Culturally sensitive research and evaluation: Advancing an agenda for Black education. In J. King (Ed.), *Black education: A transformative research and action agenda for a new century* (pp. 313–321). Mahwah, NJ: Lawrence Erlbaum Associates for the American Educational Research Association.

Tillman, L. C. (2006). Researching and writing from a position of color: Reflective notes on three research studies. *International Journal of Qualitative Studies in Education, 19*(3), 265–287.

3

The Political Paradoxes of Scientific Research in Education

*Catherine A. Lugg, Rutgers University; and
Carol F. Karpinski, Fairleigh Dickinson University*

The Bush administration's embrace of science (i.e., randomized field trials) for educational research, as well as various other policy venues, presents several intriguing political ironies. Historically, members of the political right, including the Protestant Right, have bitterly opposed wide-ranging social science experiments in public education (Diamond, 1995; 1998). Furthermore, many conservative Protestants have a particular antipathy for educational psychology (Berliner, 1997, and also Eakman, 1998). While the administration claims that No Child Left Behind will promote "teaching methods that have been proven to work. There will be no more experimenting on children with educational fads" (see U.S. Dept. of Education, n.d.), the National Research Council's recommendations concerning *fundable* federal educational research contradict part of that assertion. The second striking irony is that in other policy venues the Bush administration has launched a full-scale retreat from actual scientific research and research findings (Union of Concerned Scientists, 2004). From the environment, to energy, to health and human safety, to sexuality education, the administration has repeatedly ignored, distorted or ridiculed carefully conducted scientific research if the findings challenged its ideological assumptions or ran afoul of powerful industry groups (Weiss, 2004).

This chapter explores the underlying political tensions and paradox of the National Research Council's position on educational research (see NRC, 2002). The chapter also explores the possible political perils the current administration may encounter with its own political base if it aggressively implements a wide-ranging policy of educationally based clinical trials. Furthermore, this chapter briefly touches on the administration's approach to scientific research in other policy venues and concludes with some observations for educational research in general, and research in educational leadership in particular.

THE PROTESTANT RIGHT AND
THE FEDERAL ROLE IN EDUCATION

The early Protestant Right was marked by a strong antipathy to the desegregation of public schools, and in particular, mandatory busing to achieve desegregation (Lugg, 1996; Martin, 1996).[1] While some of their objections to school desegregation were rooted in notions of white supremacy, there was also great concern regarding the overall federal involvement with local public schools (Lugg, 1996). At the time of massive school desegregation (1969–1974), conservatives repeatedly and heatedly denounced it as a massive, unproven social science experiment imposed on millions of innocent young school children (Lugg, 1996).

These objections are rooted in conservatives' concerns about religious salvation and damnation. Conservatives and religious conservatives in particular, have been deeply worried about the possibility of governmental teaching that may conflict, and occasionally, outright contradict the religious teachings of parents (Apple, 2001; Gutmann, 1999; Lugg, 2004). Given the political nature and diverse student population of U.S. public schools, the children of Protestant conservatives are bound to be exposed to information that will contradict religious teachings—and consequently, this information may very well threaten religious faith. As a result, there can be a fair amount of tension between Protestant conservatives and school personnel, as well as the policies educators implement.

The supposed power of educational psychology and psychologists has been a special worry for Protestant conservatives. Many of their publications lamenting the ills of public education contain lurid descriptions of possible mind-control experiments inspired by totalitarian-inclined psychologists who are employed by the government (either state or more often, federal) for all manner of nefarious purposes (Berliner, 1997; and also

Eakman, 1998). These tales are spun in such a manner that is guaranteed to raise the anxiety levels of both adherents as well as concerned citizens. For example, Eakman (1998) writes:

> Today, under the cover of "mental health" and "student assessment," consultant-industry psychologists are using the government grant process as the primary vehicle for infusing *experimental therapies*, many of them medically dangerous and/or politically motivated, into school testing programs and curricula. (p. 17, emphasis added)

As the above quote indicates, this tension is particularly acute when the federal government is involved with public education through grant-funded research.

Some members of the Protestant Right have gone so far as to claim that the U.S. federal government has no legal authority whatsoever involving American public schools (Berliner, 1997; Lugg, 1996). While that claim is hyperventilated, there is a measure truth embedded in it. Historically, the federal government has played a limited role in public schools because education is not mention in the federal constitution, but is a concern of state constitutions. Education has been a local and state matter. It was not until the era of massive desegregation and the implementation of the Elementary and Secondary Education Act (ESEA now NCLB), that the federal government has played an increasingly prominent role. Much of the money and attendant regulation that the federal government currently provides involves compensatory education for low-income students, but a portion of federal dollars also supports educational research. With the money comes regulation, including increasingly stringent testing mandates for schools, and stringent methodological mandates for educational researchers.

The contemporary Protestant Right remains skeptical regarding the federal role in public schooling. Yet, for the most part, many activists have muted their staunch and long-standing criticism of the executive branch, including a historic irritant: the U.S. Department of Education (Lugg, 1996). In addition, they are strikingly silent on the federal government's embrace of randomized field trials—experimenting on our children—something that has been anathema. Instead, Protestant conservatives have aimed the vast majority of their concerns (and political activism) at the judiciary, as well as state and local boards of education. Most of their energies have been focused on science and sexuality education curricula, maintaining religious practices in public schools, and trying to expand voucher programs around the country (Lugg, 2004).

The primary reason for their silence is that the Bush administration has made the Protestant Right a central part of its political coalition. Protestant conservatives were heavily courted throughout the first term, and have received a few policy perks including the office of Faith Based Initiatives, school choice measures included in the No Child Left Behind Act, and enormous presidential access. It seems Protestant conservatives were also a positive, if somewhat over-touted, factor in the 2004 election. Nevertheless, if the Bush administration's first term is any indication as to what tangible rewards will be shown to Protestant conservatives vis-à-vis education, they should expect more symbolic than actual political perks (Lugg, 2004; Lugg, in press).

THE MEDICAL MODEL, SCIENCE, AND THE POLITICS OF EDUCATIONAL RESEARCH

> Educational research is broken in our country. . . . Educators and policy makers need objective, reliable research.
>
> —Rep. Michael Castle (as cited in Lather, 2004b, p. 16)

Starting in 1998, with the Reading Excellence Act, the federal government has moved to an increasingly narrow definition of what it considers "fundable" educational research, establishing "randomized field trials" as its Gold Standard (Lather, 2004a). By 2002, with the passage of the "Education Sciences Reform Act," the federal government clearly stated it would only fund research that followed an experimental or quasi-experimental research design (see U.S. Dept. of Education, 2002). The National Research Council (NRC), the American Educational Research Association (AERA), the Campbell Collaboration, and other organizations have attempted to define the nature of quality educational research and to use it as a springboard for effective practice (Olson & Viadero, 2002). With educational research under scrutiny and attack, the U.S. Department of Education engaged the respected, interdisciplinary, nonpartisan group NRC to make recommendations on scientific educational research. The NRC stated clearly in its report,

Scientific Research in Education, there is no best method for educational research (as cited in Cochran-Smith, 2002). Yet, the ensuing definition of quality research contained in the reauthorization of ESEA—No Child Left
Behind—departs considerably from the NRC's evaluation that stressed the
principles of scientific research, not methods. Eisenhart and Towne (2003),
participants in the NRC report formulation, assert that the definition of scientific based research in NCLB is narrower than the NRC's. NCLB also re-
moved the original definition that was in the Castle Bill, a forerunner to
NCLB, which outlined *both* quantitative and qualitative research standards.

Not surprising, the narrowing of the definition with the permutations of
what constitutes "scientific" has ignited great debate, consternation, and a
fair degree of outrage over the federal stance regarding "good" research
by educational researchers. Some scholars have dismissed this change out
of hand observing that the federal government does not insist on randomized trials in establishing its health policies concerning smoking, coal
dust, and the like (Robinson, 2003). Other researchers see this embrace of
randomized field trials as a continuation of over twenty years of assault
on educational research (Lather, 2004a, 2004b). Yvonna Lincoln and
Gaile Cannella (2004) have labeled this change in federal policy as em-
blematic of the right's move towards "mono-intellectualism," or "the
ONE way to be a proper scholar" (pp. 188–189).

What is striking is *the choice* of methodology: quasi-experimental or experimental designs (Lather, 2004a), the very methodology that would be
expected to generate considerable angst among Protestant conservatives.
As Professor Emerita of Stanford University, Nel Noddings indicated,
"Why the emphasis on experimental and quasi-experimental research,
when there's so much other good stuff out there, I don't know" (as cited in
Olson & Viadero, 2002, ¶ 21). Similarly, Gerald R. Sroufe of AERA notes,
"randomization is a powerful tool, and we should be doing more of it. But
it's a very narrow part of the scientific method" (Viadero, 2000, ¶ 4). In addition, such studies are costly, time-consuming, and common to medical
and health fields—fields that have extensive research resources when compared to education. However, funding for educational research pales in
comparison to outlays for other policy areas (Berliner & Biddle, 1995),
particularly in the post Reagan era (Lather, 2004b). In 2002, funds for educational research represented a small fraction of education expenditures,
about $564 million, as opposed to federal outlay for research for scientific,
defense, and health agencies that amounted to about $71 billion (Laitsch,

Heilman, & Shaker, 2002). In 2006, projections indicate that the U.S. Education Department would bear half of the reduction in federal "discretionary" spending (Brainard, 2004). The competition for research money creates a "market system" that can alter the body of knowledge pursued by stressing questions important to funders (Laitsch et al., 2002, p. 258).

In addition, educational research is value laden and inherently political. The U.S. public education system, by design, is deeply enmeshed in multiple and, at times, competing, political systems (local, state and federal). Consequently, research involving or about education will involve political issues, either explicitly (sometimes), or implicitly (more likely). As educational researcher Betty Malen (Cibulka, Malen, & Peterson, 1999) observed, "Political interactions can shape what (or whose) knowledge is privileged as well as what (or whose) topics of inquiry merit scholarly attention and/or governmental funding" (pp. 185–186; see also Fischer, 1990). There are also private organizations that fund research, organizations that can be very ideologically driven. Research questions pursued by "advocacy institutions" such as conservative think tanks provide a counterpoint to traditional, academic research and when their viewpoint is in synchronization with those who hold the purse strings the nature of research can be skewed (Laitsch et al, 2002). Should these organizations embrace not only a particular viewpoint but also endorse a specific methodology the effect on research and practice can be significant. For example, supporters of this supposed "gold standard" in educational research methodology argue that it can enhance classroom practice by replacing "individual experiences" or "philosophies" (Chenoweth, 2004), which critics allege are the tools of the trade for the "soft sciences," notably educational research. Moreover, in an attempt to force yet another "model" on schools, phrases borrowed from medicine such as dosages, control groups, and treatments pepper documents issued by the U.S. Department of Education as well as private educational groups (Chatterji, 2004).

Ironically, this abiding faith in the medical model may well be misplaced. Research in the "hard" sciences has had its share of missteps. For example, "corporate-sponsored drug research produced results that corroborated what the sponsor hoped to find 98% of the time" while independent researchers found support "only 79% of the time" (Laitsch et al, 2003, p. 257.) In addition, owing to the imprecise federal definition of research, some quality improvement projects in the medical field have been shielded from Institutional Review Board scrutiny resulting in concerns regarding the participants' welfare and privacy (Brainard, 2003). Furthermore, throughout the 1990s, there were numerous scandals involving "informed consent"—or the lack thereof—and the subsequent deaths of research participants, in several famous university based clinical trials. Clinical trials in medicine, until the 1990s, tended to be biased in that, in many instances, white males were viewed as the universal human. Even in medicine, clinical trials are viewed as one of many forms of research including longitudinal case studies, which can have far greater explanatory power.

Most important, the randomized field trial model utilized in "scientifically based research" ignores the distinctiveness and complexities of educational settings by advocating a methodological straight jacket (Lather, 2004b). Even proponents of randomized field trials state emphatically that by defining this sole method as providing "trustworthy evidence—reveals a myopic view of science in general and a misunderstanding of educational research in particular" (Berliner, 2002, p. 18; see also Winn, 2003). Narrowing the knowledge base by promoting the "gold standard" can be problematic for school administrators seeking federal funds and facing a limited choice of scientifically based programs of reform to adopt. Acting to assist in this choice, the U.S. Department of Education issued a nineteen-page booklet with guidelines for evidence-based research. Prepared by a nonpartisan group that supports such research, the Coalition for Evidence-Based Policy, the guide received mixed reviews primarily because of the narrow methodological focus (Viadero, 2004). However, while stressing the value of evidence-based research, the guide does acknowledge the "possible" effectiveness of comparison studies although noting how problematic they have been concerning, for example, hormone-replacement therapy. Moreover, the "pre-post" studies, common in education research, are roundly discounted (Viadero, 2004). Furthermore, in an effort to address the difficulty in randomized studies, the guide recommends a minimum sample size for schools or classes. Thus, educational research is hampered by mode of inquiry as well as by other constraints.

For example, the What Works Clearinghouse [WWC], which is managed by the U.S. Department of Education in collaboration with the American Institutes for Research and the Campbell Collaboration is billed as a "trusted source of scientific evidence of what works in education" (What Works Clearinghouse, n.d., banner). The site indicates that experts scour resources for studies that meet its strict evidence standards. While noting that the strongest research designs include randomized controlled trials, WWC eschews qualitative case studies as beyond its purview because they lack "outcome evaluations" (What Works Clearinghouse, n.d, Review Process, ¶ 1)—a statement that is patently false (see Marshall & Rossman, 1998).

With the promulgation of new federal standards concerning "rigorous" educational research, it is likely that scholarship that fails to employ an experimental design will not receive federal funding (Berliner, 2002). For the current White House, these standards also have an added benefit. This standard quickly eliminates some potentially controversial educational researchers who employ "stand point theories" like Critical Race Theory, feminist theories, queer theories, and post-structural theory, many of which employ a variety of qualitative methodologies—methodologies which may uncover political problematic structural issues like racism, class bias, sexism, and homophobia.

The Bush administration's embrace of a purported "gold standard" in scientific research is also strikingly ironic when one examines its approach to the hard sciences. There seems to be much less concern with science and scientific data. This essay now turns to other research venues.

THE POLITICS OF SCIENCE IN OTHER VENUES: THE INFORMATION QUALITY ACT[2]

> Was it something that did not have hearings? Yes. Is it something that keeps me awake at night? No. Is it something that I would do again, exactly? Yes, you bet your ass I would. I would not even think about it, okay? Sometimes you get the monkey, and sometimes the monkey gets you.
>
> —Jim Tozzi, lobbyist and architect of the
> Information Quality Act (Weiss, 2004, ¶ 52)

The larger context within which these new research directives have been formulated generates additional concerns regarding educational research. The social sciences have been buffeted by the "culture wars" for more than a decade with Protestant conservatives as part of the onslaught (see Berliner, 1997). Therefore, it is not surprising that given the present administration's link and indebtedness to the Protestant Right, as well as business and industry groups, a seemingly innocuous addition (only 237 words) to a large appropriation bill, the Information Quality Act, has increased the angst among scientists in particular and researchers in general. Ostensibly designed to assure the quality of data generated by federal agencies, the Information Quality Act of 2001 contributes to the muddle on "data selection and interpretation" (Johnson, 2004, p. 469), raises questions on the appropriation of funds for agencies, and illustrates the increasing politicization of science (MacGarity, 2004). The Information Quality Act permits interest groups, industry paid scientists, and even non-scientists, to challenge any governmental data if the objectors can produce contrary information—not data. The Act is written in such a fashion that conflicting information is broadly construed, covering "essentially anything but opinions from agency staff, thus covering far more than narrow categories of 'data' or 'science'" (see Wagner, 2004, p. 596). The Information Quality Act also covers all U.S. Government documents published prior to the Act's authorization— potentially giving industry groups carte blanche to challenge all prior data-based regulations (MacGarity, 2004; Wagner, 2004).

The brainchild of Jim Tozzi, a noted D.C. lobbyist, the Information Quality Act stands to stymie federal regulation in a sea of litigation, challenges, and data purging by validating complaints from private associations about data quality and threatening public safety with regard to environment and health. Barry L. Johnson (2004) of the Rollins School of Public Health at Emory University notes several instances in which special interest groups initiated lengthy litigation by questioning data used in government reports on climate control, mercury levels in fish, and the Army Corps of Engineers and thus delayed the implementation of policy. The Information Quality Act, by encouraging all challenges to data— either credible or not—creates the possibility that the information if deemed "flawed" will either never be published or, if it is, subsequently be purged from government Web sites and documents (McGarity, 2004). While peer review might assure "sound science," industry advocates see the Information Quality Act as a way to limit regulation by casting doubt on established safeguards or delaying the implementation of new ones. Dr. John Graham of Harvard University who has contributed to the formulation of the Information Quality Act guidelines has clearly aligned himself with industries and against environmentalists indicating that some sympathetic to the administration see the Information Quality Act as a way to eliminate costly regulations (Revkin, 2002).

Furthermore, new guidelines produced by federal agencies to assess the quality of information at hand can also put research scrutinized by peer review journals in the discard pile (McGarity, 2004; Revkin, 2002). If data are perceived as "weak" or "flawed," the federal agency in question can be placed on the proverbial political hot seat and the programs underwritten with that data stand to lose appropriations. Clearly, the government must generate data that withstand challenges about validity by supporting a process that encourages a high level of scientific inquiry. This is commendable but the value of the process is only as good as the players, their objectivity, and their integrity (MacGarity, 2004). Moreover, seemingly arbitrary limits on the nature of scientific inquiry are contradictory to such exploration. Not surprisingly, the Union of Concerned Scientists (UCS, 2004) cites examples of scientific distortion involving the invocation of the Information Quality Act, including subversion of data, manipulation of research panels in cases dealing with the Endangered Species Act and mountaintop mining to name but two instances (see also Thompson, 2003).

John Marburger III, President Bush's science adviser, denied the UCS's charges that scientists were tapped for a federal science advisory panel only if they passed a political litmus test, as well as those who engaged in peer review were receiving federal funding (Hileman, 2004; Keiger, 2004). However, the record indicates otherwise. According to the previously mentioned UCS (2004) report, "Sharon Smith, chair of the marine biology department at the Rosenstiel School of Marine and Atmospheric Science at the University of Miami states that she was summarily rejected for a position on the U.S. Arctic Research Commission—a presidential appointment—after she gave a less-than enthusiastic answer in response to a question from the White House personnel office about whether she supported President Bush" (p. 28). Similarly, Dr. Richard Myers and Dr. George Weinstock were rejected from the serving on The National Advisory Council for Human Genome Research at the National Institute of Health because they had both failed the political litmus test (UCS, 2004). There are other reports of political litmus tests across federal scientific advisory boards (see UCS, 2004; Robbins, 2003).

Consequently, in this atmosphere of managed public information—or spin—the Information Quality Act is especially problematic because it opens the door to seemingly endless industry challenges, which can delay the implementation of safeguards and given the recent alignment of the administration with industry, the Information Quality Act can further unravel environmental and medical safeguards already in play. While the Office of Management and Budget asserts that the Information Quality Act has thus far resulted in only several dozen challenges (Kaiser, 2004), one can argue that the significance of the challenges, not the number, to public health and safety remains paramount.

"Sound science" in recent memory has not been limited to peer review by scholars but partisan advocates (Mooney, 2004; McGarity, 2004). The phrase evoked frequently in the 1990s regarding the tobacco industry and the perils of secondhand smoke, the opening up of Alaska to oil and gas drilling based on "sound science," and the use of questionable pesticides to kill insects based on "sound science" signal concerns about the administration's conceptualization of science and scientific research. To a degree, the Bush administration's point of view reflects the drift from the Nixon administration, as well as the Republican party, from its ties to the science community (Thompson, 2003). Certainly, the Bush administration's predilection for "junk science" has been widely discussed with regard to the global warming debate in which environmentalists noted the distortion and elimination of data that contradicted the administration's perspective (Kennedy, 2004; see also Cohen, 2004). A former director of the National Park Service attests that "it's hard to decide what is more demoralizing about the Administration's politicization of the scientific process . . . its disdain for professional scientists working for our government or its willingness to deceive the American public" (Kennedy, 2004, ¶ 10). Likewise, the endorsement of studies funded by partisan advocates can undermine environmental policies, as was the case in the proposed development of the western Everglades for recreation (Kennedy, 2004). Relinquishing data collection to private firms with special interest connections has become commonplace in the Bush administration (Kennedy, 2004). With severe limitations on government funded science research, the research undertaken by interested partisans takes on greater prominence in any data starved field.

Regarding education, the Bush administration's idiosyncratic conception of science triggered a misrepresentation of data in a reappraisal of a study on vouchers by the Center for Evaluation and Education Policy at Indiana University. While the research report concluded that there were no

but the hue and cry for more scientific and rigorous research may forestall the utilization of information already in the knowledge base (Berliner, as cited in Olson, 2002), particularly information that contradicts the educational philosophy and theology of the Protestant Right.

Although there is considerable support from educational researchers for a mix of methodological approaches (Gardner, 2002; Gribbons & Herman, 1997; Winn, 2003) and for "multiple viewpoints (i.e., paradigmic, epistemological, theoretical, conceptual, and methodological)" (Johnson, 2003), the selection of research data based on its adherence to quantifiable results can undermine programs where results are not readily defined in a short time span nor easily measured. Interestingly, this places advocates of some educational initiatives on the same trajectory as medical researchers who are unhappy with the current stringent measuring tools (Morgan, 2002). Arriving at a precise measure of the success of federal programs, regardless of agency, has been problematic since the introduction of the Planning, Programming, and Budgeting System in 1966 under President Lyndon Johnson. Presidents Nixon, Carter, Clinton, and George W. Bush have acted to insure accountability but a precise instrument remains elusive. The Performance Assessment Rating Tool used to evaluate current programs indicates that more than half of federal programs have not shown results (Rating the performance, n.d.). One educational program, Upward Bound that has assisted disadvantaged students since the 1960s in their pursuit of a college education, has been under attack for several years owing to a study that indicated that it did not *measurably* increase college attendance for these students. Therefore, Upward Bound, Talent Search, and similar initiatives in the TRIO[3] program stand to lose federal support (Field, 2005). Advocates of such programs indicate that current assessment tools fail to measure the effects on self-esteem and attitude of program participants over time (Morgan, 2002). Committed to measurable outcomes, the Bush administration is moving to extend testing to high school students at the expense of Upward Bound and similar programs (Field, 2005). The current administration's conception of science, research methodology, and its propensity to quantify success affects education in terms of not only the utility of past research and the nature of future research but also the viability of programs that the research touches.

Will this supposed "gold standard" in fact become the prototype for educational research given the current state of affairs? Such research is costly if implemented, and can limit the amount of other research. The advocacy of experimental and quasi-experimental research may also be a smokescreen to dismantle or discredit what does not suit the perspective of the administration or its power base—including the Protestant Right. As we have indicated, there are multiple ironies here that relate to the Protestant Right, which has been so critical to Bush's success. Their objections to clinical trials that treat school children like laboratory rats (in their view, see Eakman, 1998), could successfully thwart these very trials at the local level, particularly in places where activists from the Protestant Right have actively pursued school board membership. Such clinical trials would need to be approved by local school officials in addition, one would hope, to an Institutional Review Board (or Human Subjects) review. But how this "gold standard" plays out at the local level will be determined by context and issues—contexts that are far beyond federal reach.

Conflict is not new where politics dominates the process of determining "who gets what research dollars, when and how" (with apologies to Harold Lasswell). But conflict can be eviscerating for those involved, as well as occasionally invigorating. The current debate over scientific research continues as educational researchers explore extending the knowledge base and incorporating new and multiple viewpoints. Given the administration's perspective, there is the potential and, in fact, many political incentives, for dismantling long-standing programs and discrediting past and present research. The situation is particularly acute since the Bush administration faces looming budget deficits into the foreseeable future, coupled with ever rising costs of the current Iraq war and military occupation (Lugg, in press). Any funding for educational research is sure to be reduced in light of these larger and pressing political issues.

Thus, the ethics of research become paramount not only in expanding a knowledge base to help practitioners and their charges, but also in guarding knowledge that has helped to protect diversity, advance educational equity, and promote social justice. For educational research in general, and researchers who examine educational leadership in particular, the availability of federal grants will become increasingly scarce—regardless of one's own methodological orientation. It is incumbent that in an age of reduced resources, super-heated political debates, coupled with powerful political forces narrowly defining what constitutes "good" research, that we maintain our own professional prerogatives. Our professional integrity requires it and the children who attend our public schools most certainly deserve it.

NOTES

1. This chapter uses the terms Protestant right and Protestant conservatives throughout. We are referring to religiously motivated political activists. While the terms Christian Right and Religious Right are more common, they are a bit disingenuous because they obscure the point that the vast majority of these activists are Protestant. The social science research on this point is clear: The vast majority of religious activists are Protestants and tend to be either evangelical or fundamentalist in their theological orientation.

2. The Information Quality Act is also known as the Data Quality Act. In both the research and popular literature, there is a fair amount of confusion as to the actual name of the legislation in question. The correct title is "Information Quality Act."

3. The U.S. federally funded TRIO program's nomenclature is obscure and misleading. Originally it was three programs but today includes Talent Search, Students Support Services, Upward Bound, Upward Bound Mat/Science, Veterans Upward Bound, Educational Opportunity Centers, and the Ronald E. McNair Post-Baccalaureate Achievement Program.

REFERENCES

Advocates for Youth. Science or politics? (2004). *George W. Bush and the future of sexuality education in the United States.* Retrieved December 22, 2004, from htttp://www.advocatesforyouth.org/publications/factsheet/fsbush.htm.

Allington, R. L. (Ed.). (2002). *Big brother and the national reading curriculum: How ideology trumped evidence.* Portsmouth, NH: Heinemann.

Apple, M. W. (2001). *Educating the "right way": Markets, standards, God, and inequality.* New York: Routledge.

Berliner, D. C. (1997). Educational psychology meets the Christian right: Differing views of children, schooling, teaching, and learning. *Teachers College Record, 98,* 381–416.

Berliner, D. C. (2002). Educational research: The hardest science of all. *Educational Researcher, 31*(8), 18–20.

Berliner, D. C., & Biddle, B. J. (1995). *The manufactured crisis: Myths, fraud, and the attack on America's public schools.* Cambridge, MA: Perseus Books.

Brainard, J. (2003, December 13). Research-agency officials question White House's review of basic science [Electronic version]. *Chronicle of Higher Education.*

Brainard, J. (2004, May 28). Bush administration is said to plan big cuts for research and student aid in 2006 budget [Electronic version]. *Chronicle of Higher Education.*

Chatterji, M. (2004). Evidence on "What works" in education: An argument for extended-term mixed-method (ETMM) evaluation designs. *Educational Researcher, 33*(9), 3–13.

Chenoweth, K. (2004). Commentary: Knowing what works: To revolutionize education, we first have to understand it [Electronic version]. *Education Week, 23.*

Cibulka, J. G., Malen, B., &. Peterson, P. E. (1999). Three researchers reflect: Vignettes and verities. *Educational Policy, 13*(1–2), 180–198.

Cochran-Smith, M. (2002). Editorial: What a difference a definition makes. *Journal of Teacher Education, 53*(3), 187–189.

Cohen, M. J. (2004). George W. Bush and the Environmental Protection Agency: A midterm appraisal. *Society & Natural Resources, 17*(1), 69–88.

Diamond, S. (1995). *Roads to dominion: Right-wing movements and political power in the United States.* New York: Guilford Press.

Diamond, S. (1998). *Not by politics alone: The enduring influence of the Christian Right.* New York: Guilford Press.

Eakman, B. K. (1998). *Cloning of the American mind: Eradicating morality through education.* Lafayette, LA: Huntington House.

Eisenhart, M., & Towne, L. (2003, October). Contestation and change in national policy on "scientifically based" education research [Electronic version]. *Educational Researcher,* pp. 31–38.

Field, K. (2005, January 24). Bush's budget for 2006 may propose killing 2 key programs for college access [Electronic version]. *Chronicle of Higher Education, 51.*

Fischer, F. (1990). Organizations as political systems: The managerial bias in critical perspective. In F. Fischer (Ed). *Technocracy and the politics of expertise* (pp. 269–298). Newbury Park, CA: Sage.

Foster, L. (2002). Review of the book *Policy research in educational settings: Contested terrain* [Electronic version]. *Teachers College Record, 104*(2).

Gardner, H. (2002). Commentary: The quality and qualities of educational research [Electronic version]. *Education Week, 22.*

Gribbons, B., & Herman, J. (1997). *True and quasi-experimental designs* [Electronic version]. Washington DC: ERIC Clearinghouse on Assessment and Evaluations. Retrieved January 2, 2005, from http://chiron.valdosta.edu .whuitt/files/expdesigns.html (ERIC Document Reproduction Service No. ED421483).

Gutmann, A. (1999). *Democratic education.* Princeton: Princeton University Press.

Hileman, B. (2004, April 7). Marburger responds to allegations that White House politicizes science [Electronic version]. *Chemical & Engineering News.*

Johnson, B. L. (2003). Those nagging headaches: Perennial issues and tensions in the politics of education field [Electronic version]. *Educational Administration Quarterly, 39*(1), 41–67.

Johnson, B. L. (2004). Editorial: Is there quality in the Data Quality Act of 2001? *Human and Ecological Risk Assessment, 10,* 469–472.

Kaiser, J. (2004). Trickle, not flood of *Data Quality* requests. *Science* 304(5873), 941. Retrieved January 2, 2005, from http://web33.epnet.com/citation.asp?.

Keiger, D. (2004). Political science. *Johns Hopkins Magazine.* Retrieved November 15, 2004, from http://www.jhu.edu/~jhumag/1104web/polysci.html.

Kennedy, R. F., Jr. (2004, March 8). The junk science of George W. Bush. *The Nation.* Retrieved March 5, 2004, from http://www.truthout.org/docs_04/ 030204C.shtml.

Laitsch, D., Heilman, E.E., & Shaker, P. (2002). Teacher education, pro-market policy and advocacy research. *Teaching Education, 13*(3), 251–271.

Lather, P. (2004a). Scientific research in education: A critical perspective. *Journal of Curriculum and Supervision, 20*(1), 14–30.

Lather, P. (2004b). This IS your father's paradigm: Government intrusion and the case of qualitative research in education. *Qualitative Inquiry, 10*(2), 15–34.

Lincoln, Y. S., & Cannella, G. S. (2004). Qualitative research, power, and the radical right. *Qualitative Inquiry, 10*(2), 175–201.

Lugg, C. A. (1996). *For God and country: Conservatism and American school policy.* New York: Peter Lang.

Lugg, C. A. (2003). Sissies, faggots, lezzies and dykes: Gender, sexual orientation and the new politics of education. *Educational Administration Quarterly, 39*(1), 95–134.

Lugg, C. A. (2004). One nation under God? Religion and the politics of education in a post-9/11 America. *Education Policy, 18*(1), 169–187.

Lugg, C. A. (in press). *Some thoughts on the Bush administration's second term.* Politics of Education Bulletin.

Manzo, K. K. (2002). Some educators see reading rules as too restrictive [Electronic version]. *Education Week, 21.*

Marshall, C., & Rossman, G. (1998). *Designing qualitative research* (3rd ed.). Thousand Oaks, CA: Sage Publications.

Martin, W. (1996). *With God on our side: The rise of the religious right in America*. New York: Broadway Books.

McGarity, T. O. (2004). Our science is sound science and their science is junk science: Science-based strategies for avoiding accountability and responsibility for risk-producing products and activities. *Kansas Law Review, 52*, 897–937.

Metcalf, K. K. (1998). Commentary: Advocacy in the guise of science [Electronic version]. *Education Week, 18*.

Mooney, C. (2004, February 29). Beware "sound science." It's doublespeak for trouble. *Washington Post*, p. B02.

Morgan, R. (2002, May 3). Upward Bound's slippery slope [Electronic version]. *Chronicle of Higher Education.*

National Research Council (NRC) Committee Scientific Principles for Education Research (2002). *Scientific research in education.* R. J. Shavelson & L. Towne (Eds.). Washington, DC: National Academy Press.

Olson, L., & Viadero, D. (2002). Law mandates scientific base for research [Electronic version]. *Education Week, 21.*

Rating the performance of federal programs. (n.d.). Retrieved January 17, 2005, from http://www.whitehouse.gov/omb/budget/fy2004/performance.html.

Revkin, A. C. (2002, March 21). Law revises standards for scientific study [Electronic version]. *New York Times.*

Robbins, A. (2003, December 7). Science for special interests [Electronic version]. *Boston Globe.*

Robinson, D. H. (2004, April). An interview with Gene Glass. *Educational Researcher, 33*(3), 26–30.

Shilts, R. (1987). *And the band played on: Politics, people and the AIDS epidemic*. New York: St. Martin's Press.

Thompson, N. (2003, July/August). Science friction: The growing- and dangerous-divide between scientists and the GOP [Electronic version]. *Washington Monthly.*

Tyack, D. (1974). *The one best system: A history of American urban education.* Cambridge, MA: Harvard University Press.

Union of Concerned Scientists. (2004). *Scientific integrity in policy making? Further investigation into the Bush administration's misuse of science.* Retrieved December 31, 2004, from http://ucsusa.org/global_environoment/rsi/page/cfm?.

U.S. Department of Education. (n.d.). *Ten facts every parent should know about the No Child Left Behind Act.* Retrieved May 5, 2004, from http://www.ed.gov/nclb/overview/tenfacts/index.html.

U.S. Department of Education (2002). Educational Sciences Reform Act [ESRA] of 2002. Retrieved December 2, 2004, from http://www.ed.gov/policy/rschstat/ leg/PL107-279.pdf.

Viadero, D. (2000). Definition of "research" raises concerns [Electronic version]. *Education Week, 19.*

Viadero, D. (Ed.). (2004). Dept. issues practical guide to research-based practice [Electronic version]. *Education Week, 23.*

Wagner, W. E. (2004). The practice of epidemiology and administrative agency created science: Importing *Daubert* to administrative agencies through the Information Quality Act. *Journal of Law & Policy, 12*, 589–617.

What Works Clearinghouse. (n.d.). Review process. Retrieved January 21, 2005, from http://www.w-w-c.org/reviewprocess/notmeetscreeens.html.

Weiss, R. (2004, August 16). "Data quality" law is nemesis of regulation [Electronic version]. *Washington Post.*

Winn, W. (2003). Research methods and types of evidence for research in educational technology. *Educational Psychology Review, 15*(4), 367–373.

4

"Scientific" Research and the New Narrative for Educational Leadership[1]

Gail C. Furman, Washington State University

What is the nature and purpose of educational leadership in schools? This is a critical question to address when considering the type of research that might be most useful in understanding and improving leadership practice. In other words, how leadership is conceptualized and how this conceptualization has shifted over the years have major implications for planning and conducting research. Interestingly, however, educational researchers often neglect this fundamental need to match conceptualization or construct to research approach.

While there is certainly no universal agreement on the nature of educational leadership, there has been a distinct shift in the literature over the last several decades. In essence, this shift has been away from the scientific management perspective, toward a new narrative that focuses more on moral leadership, including the moral purposes of leadership practice (Furman, 2003). This shift has accelerated in the last ten years with increased attention to the relationships among leadership practice and various "moral goods" in schools, e.g., learning for all children, democratic community, and social justice (Grogan, 2002; Marshall, 2004; Murphy, 1999).

The recent work of a national research task force jointly sponsored by American Education Research Association (AERA) Division A, University Council for Educational Administration (UCEA), and the Laboratory for Student Success at Temple University helps to illustrate this shift in conceptions of educational leadership. The task force's purpose was to develop a "clear and compelling agenda for future research in educational leadership" (Firestone & Riehl, 2003); to this end, project co-directors William Firestone and Carolyn Riehl invited a panel of sixteen scholars to review and analyze the research around various leadership topics, including the links between leadership practice and student learning, and to propose future research agenda around these topics. Altogether, the panel generated nine papers, which have been presented at national conferences and compiled in a 2006 book (Firestone & Riehl).

Project codirector Carolyn Riehl presented a preliminary analysis of the task force work at the 2004 AERA conference and noted several interesting trends that cut across the various topics. First, the papers generally take a "constructivist" view of educational leadership, that is, that leadership is not only "distributed" among educators in specific school sites but is actually "constructed" by them as they work together toward their goals; thus, leadership is seen by many of these scholars as a shared, context-bound, dynamic phenomenon, which responds to site-specific conditions. In addition, the papers suggested that this constructed leadership is aimed at meaningful goals that are value-driven, e.g., learning for all children, social justice, and so on. In one of the task force papers, Furman and Shields (2006) further argued that leadership aimed at the value-driven goal of promoting social justice in schools is also multidimensional; that is, such leadership involves moral aspects, community-building work, a pedagogical focus, purposeful transformative practices, and so on. Related to these views of leadership, many panelists called for an "engaged" form of research that attends to normative issues, that may be specifically interventionist and advocacy oriented, and that takes into account the perspectives of the marginalized in specific research sites as well as the multidimensionality of leadership practice. Further, this engaged form of research should be "just and democratic" (Furman & Shields, 2006) in itself, aimed at benefiting research participants as well as the researchers, if it is focused on moral issues such as social justice in schools.

In essence, this "new" narrative of educational leadership requires a different way of thinking about the type of research that is needed to further understandings of leadership practice. It suggests research approaches that are incompatible with the version of "scientific" research privileged in current federal education policy.[2] To date, however, there has been very little explicit analysis of the applicability of these scientific research guidelines to research on educational leadership.

Given the emerging new narrative for educational leadership vis-à-vis the current debates about scientific research in education, this chapter will explore the following topics: the "old" narrative in educational leadership and its relation to scientific research; the emerging "new" narrative; and the implications of the new narrative for research in the field.

THE "OLD" NARRATIVE OF EDUCATIONAL LEADERSHIP AND "SCIENTIFIC" RESEARCH

The "old" narrative of educational leadership had its beginnings early in the twentieth century when the nascent field of educational administration imported management perspectives from the successful and admired world of business and industry (Murphy, 2005). "Taylorism," in particular, was one perspective that dominated business thinking at the time. Originating in the work of Frederick Winslow Taylor, an industrial efficiency expert with an engineering background, "the Taylor system" focused on efficiency, productivity, and "scientific management" in organizations. According to Taylor, through "scientific" time and motion studies, the "one best way" (most efficient) for doing any particular job could be determined, all similar jobs could then be "standardized," and, through proper "scientific management," workers could be motivated and/or compelled to perform to standard, vastly increasing productivity (Callahan, 1962; Gross, 1964). Taylorism's influence spread throughout the Western industrial world of the twentieth century and continues to hold sway in post-industrial, global corporate society, though it has morphed over time into various "neo-Taylorist" perspectives. Indeed, as Shipps (2006) states, Taylorism has become a "world-wide narrative of compelling detail."

In the early years of the field of educational administration, the Taylorist narrative had a powerful influence on understandings of school efficiency and administrators' roles. The Taylorist administrator would be able to "produce the greatest learning with the least effort" (Shipps, 2006) through detailed management and coordination of the staff, physical plant, resources, students, and so on. As the field of educational administration developed, this Taylorist mind-set continued to have a powerful influence on conceptions of leadership as well as educational policy and practice, though the "cult of efficiency" it spawned in education was roundly criticized by many scholars (e.g., Callahan, 1962; English, 1994, 2003; Gamson, 2004). Today, though few educators would think of themselves as "Taylorists" per se, the mind-set remains a subtle but powerful force in the field, affecting policy and practices, and continuing to co-opt educators into the Taylorist thinking that underlies such policies. For example, in the current standards-based/accountability policy environment, various mechanisms hold educators accountable for measurable student learning outcomes. For administrators, the implication of this accountability assumption is that, through ever more efficient and effective management (e.g., "data-based" decision making), they can "produce" results in the form of ever higher student achievement scores (e.g., Schmoker, 1999). Thus, much of the contemporary thinking on education and school reform continues to be driven by "Taylorist" notions of productivity and scientific management.

The Taylorist slant on the nature of administrators' work had a major impact on research during the twentieth century. In fact, the concept of "scientific management" helped to shape and make credible mid-century calls for the development of an "administrative science" in education (Griffiths, 1964; Murphy, 2005). This administrative science would be based on behavioral science research tools, including the translation of concepts into measurable variables, the testing of hypotheses related to these variables, and the development of empirically supported theories to be used as the basis for prediction and control (Griffiths, 1964). This hoped-for science of school administration would lead to better understandings of organizational structure and effective administrative behavior, leading in turn to more efficient "goal attainment" in schools (Griffiths, 1964).

These interwoven perspectives—Taylorism and administrative science—shaped the research agenda on school administration and leadership for many years. For the most part, this research focused on (a) *who* does leadership, i.e., the individuals who occupy administrative roles in schools, spawning studies on effective leaders and their "traits" (e.g., intelligence, energy, confidence, integrity, flexibility, charisma); (b) *what* leaders do, leading to research on roles, tasks, functions, and job satisfaction; and (c) *how* leaders do leadership; this third category is by far the largest, taking in studies on the "interiority" or mental processes of leadership (e.g., decision making, problem-solving, thinking/reflection, motivations), and studies on the "exteriority" or observable actions of leadership (e.g., leadership styles and behaviors, participative/shared leadership, transactional leadership, transformational leadership) (Furman, 2003).

While these strands of research have generated many valuable findings over the years (see Leithwood & Riehl, 2006, for one overview), some critics argue that, overall, the "outcomes of the quest for a science of administration were considerably less robust than had been anticipated" (Murphy, 1999, p. 16) and that scientific approaches have not "provided the explanatory or predictive power of either understanding or advancing the field . . . to solve the myriad of political, moral, and technological dilemmas the schools face in late twentieth-century America" (pp. 230–231). Scholars point out specific weaknesses in this research base, including an overemphasis on a "heroic" notion of leadership as practiced by individuals in administrative positions (Heifetz, 1994; Lambert et al., 1995) and an overly generalized "meta-narrative" of leadership that fails to consider the unique contexts in which school leadership is practiced (English, 2003). In addition, perhaps the most damning criticism is the functionalist or value neutral stance of this research toward the "goodness" of the present educational system and the moral purposes of leadership practice (Murphy, 1999; Scheurich & Skrla, 2003). In other words, these approaches to understanding and studying leadership are largely silent in regard to the *purposes* of leadership practice, that is, what goals are most worthy to pursue in schools. Indeed, the implied goal throughout this body of work is efficiency in the production of measurable student outcomes; this goal as well as the educational system itself is not adequately critiqued in regard to moral issues such as social justice and equity (Starratt, 2003). The result is that the findings of such research tend to perpetuate the status quo of the system. Leaders who are "effective" given current structures, policies, and practices are studied, and the results of such studies are presented as models for leadership practice in what remains a closed system. As Larson and Murtadha (2002) state, "An enduring allegiance to theories of leadership oriented toward maintaining stability through universal theories and hierarchical visions of schooling has maintained inequity in education" (p. 137).

In sum, given its mechanistic, efficiency/productivity orientation to administration, the "old" Taylorist narrative of school leadership goes hand-in-glove with the hope for an "administrative science" and the use of "scientific" research methods. If it is assumed that administrators can, through their leadership practices, create more efficient and productive schools (goal attainment), then it makes sense to seek out the underlying cause-effect relationships, that is, what actions, decisions, and behaviors can administrators engage in (independent variables) that will produce the desired outcomes (dependent variables) most efficiently? Taylorism, then, seems to be a specter haunting the current federal take on "scientific research." If these federal requirements were applied to research on school leadership, the implication is that studies would need to test whether "X" leadership actions would lead to "Y" measurable outcomes. In this paradigm, then, understandings of leadership practice are reduced to the measurable relationships among variables. The great sociologist C. Wright Mills (1959) long ago pointed out one of the dangers in this approach to social science—*abstracted empiricism*—in which social theory becomes restricted to statistically significant relationships among sets of measurable variables.

TOWARD A "NEW" NARRATIVE OF EDUCATIONAL LEADERSHIP

In contrast to the Taylorist/administrative science view of leadership, a new narrative has been gradually emerging in the field, greatly accelerated by recent concerns with specific "moral goods" in schools, such as learning for all children, social justice, and democratic community (Furman, 2003; Murphy, 1999). The themes of this new narrative include a recognition of the richness and complexity of local school contexts in which leadership is practiced and, therefore, of the richness and complexity of leadership practice in response to these contexts; a view of leadership as a shared, distributed, and "constructed" phenomenon rather than a role attribute of those in administrative positions; and a foregrounding of the *why* of leadership practice, that is, the moral purposes to which it is and should be directed. Many scholars are contributing to these developing themes.

Schön (2001) describes complex environments like schools as a landscape of "messy, indeterminate, problematic situations" characterized by "complexity and uncertainty" (p. 186) and holds that professional practice in such contexts relies on a "core of artistry" (Schön, 1987, p. 13). Similarly, Goldring and Greenfield (2002) state, "The context of educational systems is complex, dynamic, and fluid, suggesting numerous scenarios that could influence the ways in which leaders enact their roles and manage dilemmas" (p. 15). English (1994, 2003), adds that school leadership is more of a "performance art" than a science, while Heifetz (1994) characterizes leadership as "adaptive work" that must respond to unpredictable challenges within unique contexts. These views suggest that seeking a meta-narrative for effective leadership practice that is generalizable across multiple school contexts is futile. Leadership is, instead, a dynamic, creative, and unpredictable response to a fluid, dynamic, and unpredictable environment.

Other scholars have convincingly portrayed leadership as a participative, shared or "distributed" phenomenon that can flourish when it is promoted and supported (Firestone, 1996; Leithwood & Duke, 1998; Pounder, Ogawa, & Adams, 1995; Smylie, Conley, & Marks, 2002; Spillane, Halverson, & Diamond, 2001). In this view of leadership, "authority and influence are available potentially to any legitimate stakeholders in the school based on their expert knowledge, their democratic right to choose, their critical role in implementing decisions, or a combination of the three" (Leithwood & Duke, 1998, p. 38). In other words, leadership "permeates organizations rather than residing in particular people or formal positions of authority"(Smylie, Conley, & Marks, 2002, p. 167). Other scholars deepen the idea of distributed leadership by noting that leadership is actually "constructed" by the multiple participants in a particular setting through their ongoing relationships. Watkins (1989), for example, posits that leadership is a "processual dialectic relationship" that "arises out of the constructions and actions of both the leaders and the followers. Thus leadership is a social construction of reality which involves an ongoing interaction" (pp. 27–28). Lambert and her colleagues (Lambert et al., 1995) have further elaborated the theory of "constructivist leadership," defining it as "the reciprocal processes that enable participants in an educational community to construct meanings that lead toward a common purpose about schooling" (p. 29). They add, "Since leadership is viewed as essentially the enabling reciprocal processes among people, leadership becomes manifest within the relationships in a community, manifest in the spaces, the fields among participants, rather than in a set of behaviors performed by an individual leader" (pp. 32–33).

Complementing these views on distributed/constructivist leadership, a rich body of work specific to teacher leadership has been recently emerging (see Smylie, Conley, & Marks, 2002; and York-Barr & Duke, 2004, for recent reviews). Ironically, Wheatley (1994) calls the growing emphasis on these relational aspects of leadership the "*new* scientific management," since it reflects new scientific discoveries of the "seamless web" of the "quantum universe" (p. 68). The distributed/constructivist view of leadership suggests that earlier understandings of school leadership have been severely limited by a too-narrow focus on individuals in formal authority positions; new understandings are needed that explore more fully the relational and distributed nature of leadership practice.

Still other scholars foreground the moral dimensions of school leadership practice. Goldring and Greenfield (2002), for example, state that the "moral dimensions of educational leadership and administration" constitute one of the special conditions that make administering schools "different from such work in other contexts" (pp. 2–3), while Sergiovanni (1996) argues that schools are "moral communities" requiring a new type of leadership based in "moral authority" (p. 57). Deepening the notion of moral leadership, some scholars focus specifically on the *moral purposes* of leadership practice. Fullan (2003) states, "the only goal worth talking about" in schools is the "moral purpose of the highest order . . . having a system where all students learn" (p. 29). Lees (1995) argues that school leadership is based in a "moral imperative to promote democracy, empowerment, and social justice" (p. 225). And English (1994) adds, "Moral leadership asks questions about *ends*. It asks questions such as, 'Who benefits from schools as they now exist?' and 'Who does not benefit from schools as they now exist?'" (p. 231, emphasis in original). Nicely summarizing this view, Scheurich and Skrla (2003) state,

> The most important characteristic of a leader—whether a principal, teacher leader, counselor, or custodian . . . is that this person has developed a strong ethical or moral core focused on equity and excellence as the only right choice for schools in a democracy. For this person, this is an indomitable belief, and indomitable commitment. (p. 100)

Each of these writers unabashedly chooses specific *ends* or moral purposes as the critical goal of leadership practice in schools. Thus, while

Strike (1999) cautions educators to think in terms of moral pluralism, because in a pluralistic society various "moral goods" legitimately play out in schools, the new narrative of leadership seems to be converging on specific "moral goods" such as social justice, equity, and democracy as the most critical needs in today's schools (Furman & Shields, 2006).

To provide a scaffolding for thinking about leadership vis-à-vis these critical moral purposes, Furman and Shields (2006) developed a framework for understanding leadership practice that is aimed specifically at the moral purposes of promoting social justice and democratic community in schools. Drawing on multiple sources related to these concepts,[3] Furman and Shields (2006) identify five critical dimensions of leadership practice: (1) *ethical and moral,* (2) *communal and contextual,* (3) *processual,* (4) *transformative,* and (5) *pedagogical.* The *ethical and moral* dimension recognizes that educational leaders must operate from a deeply held ethical "core" and have a sense of commitment to working for specific moral purposes in schools. The *communal and contextual* dimension reflects the distributed or shared nature of leadership, and further suggests that collectively, this distributed leadership is context-based—it is constructed by the members of a community in the midst of their unique local context. Relatedly, the *processual* dimension captures the "dialogic" nature of leadership and the need for continual striving toward moral purposes through the communal processes of "authentic participation." In other words, working toward important moral purposes is a continual process and depends on the crucial communal processes that are in place. The *transformative* dimension suggests that leadership for social justice and democratic community is necessarily oriented toward social change; transformative leadership practice thus works for the transformation of social conditions through problematizing existing structures and practices and imagining and constructing new institutional possibilities. Finally, the *pedagogical* dimension explicitly recognizes the importance of the core work of schools—curriculum and instruction—in working for critical moral purposes, such as social justice. While the pedagogical dimension is often neglected in discussions of social transformation, both the content of the curriculum and how it is delivered have an enormous impact on educators' and students' awareness of and actions in regard to social issues in schools and society. Thus, to achieve their moral purposes, educational leaders need to critique and possibly reorient the school's pedagogical practices.

Pulling these strands together, the new narrative of educational leadership recognizes that education is fundamentally a moral and social endeavor and, therefore, that leadership is primarily a moral and relational practice aimed at specific moral ends; further, this leadership practice is continually constructed anew through the interactions and relationships of multiple participants in unique and dynamic school contexts. This new construct of school leadership has major implications for the type of research that might be most useful in the field. In essence, it suggests new directions for research that are incompatible with the version of scientific research privileged in current federal education policy. The federal scientific research approach, when applied to educational leadership, assumes without critique that efficiency and productivity are the goals of school leadership, that leadership can be reduced to observable and replicable practices, and that these practices, once scientifically identified, can be generalized to multiple schools contexts. In contrast, the new narrative implies a more holistic, alternative research approach that recognizes the creative, moral, and context-specific nature of educational leadership. The next section turns to specific ideas for such research approaches.

IMPLICATIONS FOR RESEARCH

What are the implications of the new narrative for research on educational leadership? Three general implications are immediately apparent. First, if the practice of leadership is a creative, dynamic, and multidimensional response to the conditions and needs in specific school contexts, then it is likely futile to search for generalized meta-narratives of leadership practice applicable across contexts. Instead, it is critical to study leadership *in situ* (Greenfield, 2004), as it is actually practiced, and to concomitantly fully describe and take into account the context to which it is responding. Second, if leadership practice is inherently distributed across and constructed by multiple actors in any school setting, then it is a mistake to focus studies *primarily* on individuals in formal leadership positions, and to base understandings of leadership on such studies, one of the weaknesses of traditional research in the field. Rather, studies should explore how shared/constructed leadership plays out in specific school contexts, that is, what members of the school community (writ large) participate in this shared leadership practice, how do they participate, and why? Third, if leadership is fundamentally a moral endeavor guided by moral purpose, then these purposes, as they are both held by individuals and "constructed" collectively in specific school contexts, need to be more deeply explored and made explicit. The goal of such research is not to develop a leadership meta-narrative that is intended to guide practice across school contexts, with the goal of increasing measurable student achievement; rather, the goal is to enhance understandings of *possibilities* for the construction of a *morally grounded* leadership practice in a wide variety of contexts.

These general implications lead, in turn, to more specific methodological implications. To study both context and practice in depth obviously requires thorough, multilevel field studies that explore multiple dimensions of context (e.g., structure, policies, practices, and culture) as well as multiple dimensions of practice. Further, such in-depth studies should not be guided by a priori assumptions regarding *who* practices leadership in a particular setting. Rather, one of the purposes of such studies is to unearth the distributed nature of leadership in any particular context, for example, to "map" the construction and practice of leadership across multiple actors in any site. In addition, the need to explore and make explicit the moral purposes underlying leadership practice suggests that such multilevel field studies should include a phenomenological component, that is, they need to delve into individuals' intentions, motivations, commitments, and experiences as they construct their leadership practice in response to local needs, and, in turn, how they share these constructions and work with others to collectively construct communal moral commitments and leadership actions.

These specific implications for methods suggest an additional consideration—that the research act itself should be "just and democratic" if it is intended to explore moral leadership practice (Furman & Shields, 2006; Griffiths, 1998). Just and democratic research studies benefit the participants as well as the researchers and attempt to overcome the privileged status of certain participants (Griffiths, 1998). For example, to explore the phenomenon of shared leadership, a just and democratic study would not be guided or limited by traditional, hierarchical notions of leadership, nor by the typical "one-up" status of researchers; that is, an effort would be made *not* to privilege certain voices as more authoritative or to use one's privileged researcher status to overly dictate the contours of a study. Instead, an effort would be made to encourage and elicit as many voices as possible in a particular context and to engage with participants as equals. To illustrate, in any particular school setting, those most visibly involved in leadership practice and, therefore most likely to be included in a study, may convincingly articulate their views on "social justice" needs in their setting; but, other individuals who may be typically silent, possibly marginalized, might take a different view. Perhaps the typically silent individuals can point to justice issues that are *not* being addressed through the leadership practices, perspectives, and actions of the most "visible" or privileged leaders. Including the usually silent voices in the data would be crucial to understanding social justice issues in that setting.

One way to approach the phenomenological aspect of such research is to engage participants in a type of self-study (Bullough & Pinnegar, 2001; Feldman, 2003), in which individuals reflect on who they are as educators, the decisions and actions they take, and the impact of these actions on others. This self study is "moral work" because it has a "normative, teleological component—we don't want to just study our practice, we want to improve it in a particular direction that will affect what happens in our . . . schools" (Feldman, 2003, p. 27). Although self-study is a "mongrel: The study is always of practice, but at the intersection of self and other, and its methods are borrowed" (Bullough & Pinnegar, 2001, p. 13), typical methods include the "keeping of journals in written or video formats [and] the writing of autobiographies" (p. 13), or any other procedure that helps the individual understand and reflect upon personal values, motivations, biases, and practices.

Another specific approach that is promising is "conversation as method" (Thompson & Gitlin, 1995). This approach draws from feminist standpoint theory, which seeks to avoid reproducing "existing power relations" by imposing "a direction on educational inquiry" (p. 2). Instead, conversation as method focuses on the development of "we" relationships in inquiry, that is, inquiry is not just about knowledge production but is also about the relationship itself. Thompson and Gitlin (1995) state, "Conversation as method becomes a significant alternative to other progressive approaches to inquiry . . . insofar as participants can assume not only that they will look out for one another's interests but also that the relationship is a good in itself" (p. 17). Furthermore, conversation as method "refers to a process rather than a procedure" (p. 17); instead of conducting inquiry according to assumptions about accepted practices, conversation allows for "experimental shifts" in the relationship, shifts that can lead to creative directions for growth. In these ways, conversation as method can lead to what Thompson and Gitlin (1995) call reconstructed knowledge—a form of knowledge that "looks to create spaces in which relationships among the [research] participants are realigned, shifting the balance and authority and thereby challenging the ways in which institutional relations and local actions construct what is important in these relationships" (p. 7). Thus, conversation as method extends and deepens the call for "hearing from" oppressed or marginalized groups to a focus "on relations with members of groups other than one's own" (p. 15). In other words, conversation as method is a relational process through which both researchers and researched can be transformed in certain ways and engage in action toward new possibilities. It is, thus, an "advocacy" approach to research.

To summarize, research approaches that are compatible with the new narrative of educational leadership include in-depth field studies that involve phenomenological components, that help participants in research sites to study themselves, and that honor the relational and transformative potential of the research act itself. Unlike the purpose of the "randomized" trial approach to "scientific" research privileged in current federal policy—which is to identify replicable practices with a cause-effect relationship to measurable student achievement—the purpose of these leadership field studies is to create new understandings of the possibilities for the construction of a morally grounded leadership practice in today's schools.

CONCLUSION

It may seem "old hat" to once again discuss the influence of "Taylorism" on the history of the field and its continuing influence on conceptions of administration and leadership. However, my argument for doing so in this chapter is that it is extremely important to understand the underlying assumptions about the constructs that one is investigating in order to make wise choices about research methodology. My claim is that Taylorism is a specter that continues to haunt conceptions of leadership and notions of efficiency and "productivity" in schools, and that this Taylorist specter goes hand-in-glove with current federal policy on "scientific" research, which assumes that learning is a "product" and that experimental trials can lead to efficient, "replicable" treatments to boost student achievement. When and if applied to studies of school leadership, the federal approach implies that discrete leadership practices can be isolated, operationalized, and linked as a variable to the implementation of these effective "treatments" and increased student achievement.

I argue in this chapter that these Taylorist assumptions about school leadership are relics from the early days of the field, which are gradually being discredited and discarded as a new narrative emerges. The new narrative of moral leadership recognizes the unique and creative nature of leadership practice in response to unique and dynamic contexts, the shared and relational aspects of leadership, and the important moral purposes that must guide leadership practice in contemporary schools. While "scientific" research of the type privileged in federal policy may be useful for some very limited purposes in education (Maxwell, 2004), it is obviously a poor fit with the new narrative of educational leadership. Scholars in the field are working hard to explore new directions for research that can develop useful understandings about leadership practice (e.g., the work of the AERA/UCEA research task force discussed at the beginning of this chapter). Hopefully, new approaches to research, such as those described in this chapter, will help develop new understandings of the possibilities for a morally grounded leadership practice in schools. The needs in contemporary schools for socially just policies and practices, for communal processes of authentic participation, and for an authentic pedagogy, call out to us to continue this work and to avoid the distractions of federal research mandates based in anachronistic assumptions about learning and leadership.

NOTES

1. Sections of this chapter are adapted from "'Scientific' Research and Moral Leadership" (Furman, 2006) and "How Can Educational Leaders Promote and Support Social Justice and Democratic Community in Schools" (Furman & Shields, 2006).

2. I make no attempt in this chapter to provide a thorough summary or critique of current federal policy on "scientific research"; see Riehl and English in this volume and Eisenhart and Towne (2003) for a more detailed discussion of the federal guidelines.

3. See, for example, recent special issues of the *Journal of School Leadership* (Grogan, 2002) and *Educational Administration Quarterly* (Marshall, 2004), reviews by Furman and Starratt (2002) and Larson and Murtadha (2002), and Shields (2003).

REFERENCES

Bullough, R. V., & Pinnegar, S. (2001). Guidelines for quality in autobiographical forms of self-study. *Educational Researcher, 30*(3), 13–22.

Callahan, R. E. (1962). *Education and the cult of efficiency: A study of the social forces that have shaped the administration of the public schools.* Chicago: University of Chicago Press.

Eisenhart, M., & Towne, L. (2003). Contestation and change in national policy on "scientifically based" education research. *Educational Researcher, 32*(7), 31–38.

English, F. W. (1994). *Theory in educational administration.* New York: Harper-Collins.

English, F. W. (2003). *The postmodern challenge to the theory and practice of educational administration.* Springfield, IL: Charles C. Thomas.

Feldman, A. (2003). Validity and quality in self-study. *Educational Researcher, 32*(3), 26–28.

Firestone, W. A. (1996). Leadership roles or functions? In K. Leithwood, J. Chapman, D. Corson, P. Hallinger, & A. Hart (Eds.), *International handbook of educational leadership and administration* (pp. 395–418). Dordrecht, The Netherlands: Kluwer.

Firestone, W. A., & Riehl, C. (2003). Developing research to improve educational leadership: A project of Division A of the American Educational Research Association, the Laboratory for Student Success, and the University Council for School Administration. Unpublished manuscript.

Firestone, W. A., & Riehl, C. (Eds.) (2006). *A new agenda: Direction for research on educational leadership.* New York: Teachers College Press.

Fullan, M. (2003). *The moral imperative of school leadership.* Thousand Oaks, CA: Corwin.

Furman, G. (2003, Winter). The 2002 UCEA presidential address: Toward a new scholarship of educational leadership. *UCEA Review, 45*(1), 1–6.

Furman, G. C. (2006). "Scientific" research and moral leadership in schools. In D. E. Mitchell (Ed.), *New foundations for knowledge in educational administration, policy, and politics: Science and sensationalism* (pp. 129–134) Mahwah, NJ: Lawrence Erlbaum Associates.

Furman, G. C., & Shields, C. M. (2006). How can educational leaders promote and support social justice and democratic community in schools? In W. A. Firestone & C. Riehl (Eds.), *A new agenda: Directions for research on educational leadership* (pp. 181–210). New York: Teachers College Press.

Furman, G. C., & Starratt, R. J. (2002). Leadership for democratic community in schools. In J. Murphy (Ed.), *The educational leadership challenge: Redefining leadership for the 21st century* (pp. 105–133). Chicago: National Society for the Study of Education.

Gamson, D. A. (2004). The infusion of corporate values into progressive education: Professional vulnerability or complicity? *Journal of Educational Administration, 42,* 137–159.

Goldring, E., & Greenfield, W. (2002). Understanding the evolving concept of leadership in education: Roles, expectations, and dilemmas. In J. Murphy (Ed.), *The educational leadership challenge: Redefining leadership for the 21st century. One hundred-first yearbook of the National Society for the Study of Education* (pp. 1–19). Chicago: National Society for the Study of Education.

Greenfield, W. D. (2004). Moral leadership in schools. *Journal of Educational Administration, 42,* 174–196.

Griffiths, D. E. (Ed.). (1964). *Behavioral science and educational administration. The sixty-third yearbook of the National Society for the Study of Education.* Chicago: National Society for the Study of Education.

Griffiths, M. (1998). *Educational research for social justice: Getting off the fence.* Philadelphia: Open University Press.

Grogan, M. (2002). Guest editor's introduction: Leadership for social justice. *Journal of School Leadership, 12,* 112–115.

Gross, B. M. (1964). The scientific approach to administration. In D. E. Griffiths (Ed.), *Behavioral science and educational administration. The sixty-third yearbook of the National Society for the Study of Education* (pp. 33–72). Chicago: National Society for the Study of Education.

Heifetz, R. A. (1994). *Leadership without easy answers.* Cambridge, MA: Belknap Press.

Lambert, L., Walker, D., Zimmerman, D. P., Cooper, J. E., Lambert, M. D., Gardner, M. E., & Slack, P. J. F. (1995). *The constructivist leader.* New York: Teachers College Press.

Larson, C. L., & Murtadha, K. (2002). Leadership for social justice. In J. Murphy (Ed.), *The educational leadership challenge: Redefining leadership for the 21st century* (pp. 134–161). Chicago: National Society for the Study of Education.

Lees, K. A. (1995). Advancing democratic leadership through critical theory. *Journal of School Leadership, 5*, 220–230.

Leithwood, K., & Duke, D. L. (1998). Mapping the conceptual terrain of leadership: A critical point of departure for cross-cultural studies. *Peabody Journal of Education, 73*(2), 31–50.

Marshall, C. (2004). Social justice challenges to educational administration: Introduction to a special issue. *Educational Administration Quarterly, 40*, 5–15.

Maxwell, J. (2004). Causal explanation, qualitative research, and scientific inquiry in education. *Educational Researcher, 33*(2), 3–11.

Mills, C. W. (1959). *The sociological imagination.* Oxford, UK: Oxford University Press.

Murphy, J. (1999). *The quest for a center: Notes on the state of the profession of educational leadership.* Columbia, MO: University Council for Educational Administration.

Murphy, J. (2005). Unpacking the foundations of ISLLC standards and addressing concerns in the academic community. *Educational Administration Quarterly, 41*, 154–191.

Pounder, D. G., Ogawa, R. T., & Adams, E. A. (1995). Leadership as an organization-wide phenomenon: Its impact on school performance. *Educational Administration Quarterly, 31*, 564–588.

Scheurich, J. J., & Skrla, L. (2003). *Leadership for equity and excellence.* Thousand Oaks, CA: Corwin.

Schmoker, M. (1999). *Results: The key to continuous school improvement.* Alexandria, VA: Association for Supervision and Curriculum Development.

Schön, D. (1987). *Educating the reflective practitioner: Toward a new design for teaching and learning in the professions.* San Francisco, CA: Jossey-Bass.

Schön, D. (2001). The crisis in professional knowledge and the pursuit of an epistemology of practice. In J. Raven & J. Stephenson (Eds.), *Competence in the learning society* (pp. 183–207). New York: Peter Lang.

Sergiovanni, T. J. (1996). *Leadership for the schoolhouse: How is it different? Why is it important?* San Francisco, CA: Jossey-Bass.

Shields, C. M. (2003). *Good intentions are not enough: Transformative leadership for communities of difference.* Lanham, MD: Scarecrow Press.

Shipps, D. (2006). The "science" and politics of urban educational leadership: An argument for a reorienting narrative. In D. E. Mitchell (Ed.), *New foundations for knowledge in educational administration, policy, and politics: Science and sensationalism.* Mahwah, NJ: Lawrence Erlbaum Associates.

Smylie, M. A., Conley, S., & Marks, H. M. (2002). Exploring new approaches to teacher leadership for school improvement. In J. Murphy (Ed.), *The educational leadership challenge: Redefining leadership for the 21st century* (pp. 162–188). Chicago: National Society for the Study of Education.

Spillane, J. P., Halverson, R., & Diamond, J. B. (2001). Investigating school leadership practice: A distributed perspective. *Educational Researcher, 30*(3), 23–28.

Starratt, R. J. (2003). *Centering educational administration: cultivating meaning, community, responsibility.* Mahwah, NJ: Lawrence Erlbaum Associates.

Strike, K. A. (1999). Justice, caring, and universality: In defense of moral pluralism. In M. S. Katz, N. Noddings, & K. A. Strike (Eds.), *Justice and caring: The search for common ground in education* (pp. 21–36). New York: Teachers College Press.

Thompson, A., & Gitlin, A. (1995). Creating spaces for reconstructing knowledge in feminist pedagogy. *Educational theory on the web, 45*(2), 1–28.

Watkins, P. (1989). Leadership, power and symbols in educational administration. In J. Smyth (Ed.), *Critical perspectives on educational leadership* (pp. 9–37). New York: Falmer Press.

Wheatley, M. J. (1994). *Leadership and the new science: Learning about organization from an orderly universe.* San Francisco, CA: Berrett-Koehler.

York-Barr, J., & Duke, K. (2004). What do we know about teacher leadership? Findings from two decades of scholarship. *Review of Educational Research, 74*, 255–316.

5

What's a Researcher to Do?
Insights for "Post-Anything" Researchers

*Carolyn M. Shields, University of
Illinois at Urbana–Champaign*

Education is not what the professions of certain men assert it to be. They presumably assert that they put into the soul knowledge that isn't in it, as though they were putting sight into blind eyes.

—Plato, 1968, pp. 194–195

Even today, more than twenty centuries later, "certain men" (and women) seem to believe that educational research has the potential to put sight into blind eyes, to provide the magic bullet or the fail-safe prescription for improving educational achievement, for teaching children to read, or perhaps for the introduction of more equitable education policies. Yet, despite decades of studies and a myriad of new approaches to educational research, some wonder what it is exactly that research can accomplish and how we can ever acquire the knowledge we need to improve the education we offer to our children.

There was a time when scientific research methods seemed to be clearly understood and relatively universally accepted. Regardless of whether one was conducting a study in the physical sciences or the human sciences (note the use of the term science), research seemed to be a relatively straightforward endeavor. One identified a hypothesis, developed an experiment in order to "test" it, collected and analyzed the data, and finally, proclaimed the "truth" (or lack therefore) of the hypothesis. However, when Thomas Kuhn wrote his contested, but now seminal, *Structure of Scientific Revolutions*, the term *paradigm* began to gain popularity. It became

popular to accept Kuhn's notion that a given paradigm had somehow failed
to adequately explain the phenomenon in question, and hence to call for a
new approach, a new paradigm that might function more adequately. Kuhn
(1970) writes

> scientific revolutions are inaugurated by a growing sense, often restricted to
> a narrow subdivision of the scientific community, that an existing paradigm
> has ceased to function adequately in the exploration of an aspect of nature
> to which that paradigm had previously led the way. (p. 92)

Only a few decades later, in growing recognition that previous approaches inadequately explained human phenomena, the "paradigm wars"
erupted in education. Research was no longer a simple or singular endeavor. Paradigms were "incommensurable" many asserted (see, for example, Bates, 1980; Burrell & Morgan, 1979; Greenfield, 1975; Willower;
1996). One needed to make a decision, to take a stand, and to proclaim
one's research paradigm, one that was consistent with the epistemological
and methodological positions one claimed. Before Donmoyer (1999) advanced his notion of the "big tent" that could accommodate multiple research perspectives, declaring one's approach to research frequently led to
membership in an "in" group or ostracism to an "out" group.

Early in the twenty-first century, we recognize that the new approaches
that emerged as a result of the paradigm wars did not always fulfill the
promise of being more adequate, more accurate, more correct, or indeed,
more satisfying. Moreover, in their own ways, they were as unsatisfactory
and as mystifying as their precursors. Farella (1993) introduces his book
about doing anthropology among the Navajo, by saying it is "an attack on
categorizing experience and people. Therefore it is anti social science, anti
Aristotelian, anti any sort of ownership of knowledge, anti organization or
bureaucracy. And it is opinionated, not open-minded" (pp. xiii–xiv).

He shatters what he describes as the "myth of understanding"—the social science researcher's predilection for seeking "cycles and wholes
in places where others only see independent elements" (p. 69). Farella
(1993) writes:

> So you do this social science ritual; you explain or invent these cycles and
> claim knowledge and understanding as the product, but something doesn't
> happen. No matter how correct or brilliant the explanation, it makes no dif-

ference. The understanding doesn't bring peace, in fact in many ways it makes living with tragedy even more difficult. And it also doesn't enable us to control, to bring change to the world. (p. 71)

His book is an indictment, not of the current return to "scientific" research (although it is applicable), but of social science research that aims to categorize, explain, predict and control both experiences and people. Farella's book is equally an indictment of many of the more interpretive approaches to making sense of others' experiences that he experienced in the 1980s and 1990s. And for educational researchers, he offers appropriate (if somewhat tongue-in-cheek) cautions about the claims we make about public education.

In recent years, the landscape has become even more convoluted with the emergence of the "posts"—post-modernism, post-colonialism, post-structuralism, post-positivism, post-socialism, post-foundationalism, to name a few—generally in reaction to previous stances of certitude. More recently, however, the renewed emphasis (at least in the United States) on empirical and more positivistic research has emerged as a form of backward pendulum swing, perhaps also as a reaction against the proliferation of research studies from various perspectives that some would argue have failed to have any significant impact on education. Some have taken up Farella's implicit challenge and advocated different approaches to research intended explicitly to make a difference—standpoint feminist theory (Harding, 1996) or advocacy-oriented approaches (Griffiths, 1998) for example. Others have returned to the argument, using different "post" theoretical explanations, that we cannot make a difference; indeed, that the many competing realities can neither "speak" to each other nor understand each other.

What is an educational researcher to do? How can educational research inform the praxis of educational leaders? In this paper, I examine some of the conflicts, tensions, and minefields one encounters today when approaching the task of educational research; and ultimately I attempt to provide some useful insights both for researchers and for educational leaders. To help us move forward, I briefly explore the value of two philosophical ideas (the ontological focus on relationship of Buber, 1970; Freire, 1970; Noddings, 1986; Shields & Edwards, 2005) and the ontological concept of dialogue as outlined by Bakhtin,

1986). These concepts, I argue, have the potential to provide some direction for the researcher who values and acknowledges multiple perspectives but who rejects the implicit relativism that often accompanies such a position. I end with a short discussion of why any of this discussion of research paradigms might matter to educational leaders trying to make sense of, and to act, in a very complex world.

SOME LONGSTANDING CHALLENGES

Some claim that "scientific" research is less biased, more generalizable, and hence, more useful than other, more subjective types of research. Yet, there are numerous examples of the ways in which unquestioned beliefs in the validity of scientific research have been not only inappropriate but dangerous. Gould (1981) in his *The Mismeasure of Man* describes both the science and pseudoscience of the last three centuries—approaches that were so intent on proving certain assumptions (the superiority of Caucasians for example) that data that did not support particular hypotheses were often ignored, explained away, or distorted. The craniometric studies of Morton and Broca, for example, based on erroneous measurements of skull size, posited the superiority of the white man over African Americans or American Indians; These researchers were so widely respected that their "research" stood without challenge for many decades—a testimony to the power of "scientific" research. The outcome, Gould asserts, in his 1981 revision of *The Mismeasure of Man*, has been "three centuries of racism."

Other dramatic examples of the misuse of scientific research come to mind including the devastating effects of lobotomies intended to facilitate a more normal lifestyle for those inflicted with epilepsy, of shock therapy designed to treat mental conditions such as schizophrenia, or of research conducted with prison inmates or those involved in military campaigns to test the effects of various drugs or chemical weapons. In social science, the infamous Milgram experiments continue to influence the formation of ethical guidelines for research (see Sibicky, 1996).

No less significant were the perpetuation of colonial and pathological understandings of many indigenous peoples worldwide. Consider the well-intentioned educational strategy of forbidding indigenous people to speak their own language,[1] based on research showing better acquisition of English, with greater immersion. Linda Smith (1999) writes:

> From the vantage point of the colonized, a position from which I write, and choose to privilege, the term "research" is inextricably linked to European imperialism and colonialism. The word itself, "research," is probably one of the dirtiest words in the indigenous world's vocabulary. (p. 1)

Smith (1999) goes on to assert that research is a significant site of struggle. Seen from the indigenous perspective, the struggle is between the "interests and ways of knowing of the West and the interests and ways of resisting the Other" (p. 2). Bishop and Glynn (1999) reiterate the message:

> Researchers in the past have taken the stories of research participants and have submerged them within their own stories, and re-told these reconstituted stories in a language and culture determined by the researcher. As a result, power and control over research issues . . . have traditionally been decided by the imposition of the researcher's agenda, interests, and concerns on the research process. (p. 103)

From the early brain studies, to Binet and Simon's work in the field of intelligence testing in France at the turn of the eighteenth century, to Termann's studies of giftedness,[2] to Herrnstein and Murray's famed *The Bell Curve* (1994), to the architects of the recent report on scientific research in education (the National Science Council) and the Elementory and Secondary Education Act (ESEA) (No Child Left Behind) legislation of 2002, researchers have tried to follow a scientific research path to accountability. For almost as long, other researchers have critiqued this approach and urged consideration of different issues, recognizing, as Smith (1999) states, that research itself is a site of struggle.

One of the most pervasive and longest-lasting antidotes that merged as a corrective to some of the ills of positivist, functional approaches to research and interpretation was critical theory. While much modernist thinking is characterized by a sense of the universe moving inexorably toward a better tomorrow, constantly developing, improving, and progressing, others (notably from the Frankfurt School) began to develop critiques of the existing social and economic mechanisms and the resultant marginalization and oppression of others, based on analyses of class, race, and/or economic status.

Critical theory is, as Horkeimer (as cited in Peters, Lankshear, & Olssen, 2003) maintains, not a theory with a specific content, but "comprises simply a philosophical orientation 'whose business is to hasten developments which will lead to a society without injustice'" (p. 3).

The critique of traditional approaches has most recently been so identified with the need for the liberation of oppressed groups, that it has become acceptable to advocate the silencing of voices that have traditionally been powerful, in order to listen to those who have traditionally been marginalized (see for example Boler, 2004; DeCastell, 2004). As I argue later, this position also contains inherent dangers both for educational research and for educational leadership.

It is little wonder that those who wish to embark on a research agenda have so many difficult choices and decisions to make. Likewise, one should not be surprised at the emergence of so many "post" theories, often seen as possible ways of extricating ourselves from some of the difficulties of past paradigms.

"POST" THEORIES: MORE PARADIGM PROLIFERATION

Enter post theories with their solid rejection of certainty and grand narratives, and their renewed interest in the dynamics of power. Convinced that there are multiple views of reality and that reality is "in there" (English, 2003, p. 13), postmodern research is therefore grounded personally. Not only are there multiple views of reality, but each theorist proclaims the impossibility of rationally grounding his or her theory (for such is the rejected legacy of modernism). The validity or truth (with a small "t") is to be taken on faith, for it is impossible, and contrary to "post" anything to suggest that one theory takes precedence over the other. Indeed, the implication is that all approaches and insights are equally valid, equally worthwhile and equally mysterious, some might argue.

Attempting a chronology of the "posts" would be as futile as trying to determine the starting point in the proverbial chicken and egg question. Even a summary glosses over the very real differences in understanding and nuance among the various theories and risks making untenable over-generalizations. Yet, cognizant of the dangers, I attempt here to provide a very cursory overview of some elements of the post theories that influence recent approaches to educational thinking and research. The following is provided, not in an attempt to define or explain the approaches, but simply to highlight some of the ideas that hold educational currency in this decade.

In general, in this period of "posts," the "boundaries of traditions have been blurred" (Seidman & Alexander, 2001, p. 3), the power of grand narratives (meta-narratives) has been lost, and we are always positioned in multiple and intersecting ways (p. 7). Indeed, Seidman and Alexander (in talking about Lyotard) claim, "Post-modern culture is characterized not by the loss of belief but by the acceptance of the plurality of beliefs without the need—or credible effort—to create a hierarchy of truth" (p. 13).

English (2003) claims that "postmodernism's greatest enemy is *certitude*" (p. 3). It rejects, not only claims of "Truth," but also, positions of exclusivity, and singular interpretations of past events—hence post-colonialism rejects prior colonial interpretations; post-feminism rejects previous decontextualized analyses related to gender; post-foundationalism rejects the possibility of foundational knowledge or disciplinary claims, and so forth. Burbules (1993) sums up the "notoriously vague term" *postmodernism*, by identifying assaults on hierarchy, tradition, and uniformity. In other words, he says that three issues that have been highlighted in post writings are the "centrality of an analysis of power and hierarchy as the basic dynamics of social and political organization," "the irreducible plurality of cultural world views," and a rejection of the intellectual aim of attempting to find "common underlying principles, generalizable rules, universal definitions as the sign of theoretical coherence and credibility" (pp. 2–3). Post theories in general call for the deconstruction of almost everything—texts, discourses, power relations, truth claims, identities, and prior beliefs.

"Post" thinking, therefore, raises questions about such important issues as ethics, justice, truth, identity, globalization, and civil society. Perhaps most influenced by Foucault's (2001) concepts of genealogy and archeology, it brings a renewed recognition of "the *local* character of criticism" (p. 69). The acknowledgment of the importance of both historical contexts and local particularities provides a compelling argument for the existence of "subjugated knowledges"—"knowledges that have been disqualified as inadequate to their task or insufficiently elaborated" (p. 70). These knowledges have in the past been discounted, at least in part, because of the dominance of functionalist and positivist interpretations and approaches. Foucault

(2001) states powerfully that "it is really against the effects of the power of a discourse that is considered to be scientific that the genealogy must wage its struggle" (p. 71).

Since Foucault's important critique of the power of dominant discourses, many voices have joined the struggle to liberate knowledge from positivist, and pseudo-scientific discourses that have tended to both decontextualize and reify it. Hall (2001), in speaking about Gramsci's interpretation of hegemony emphasizes that it is "never a permanent state of affairs and never uncontested. . . . Hegemony is always the (temporary) mastery of a particular theatre of struggle" (p. 97).

Assertions that there are no universal truths (except that none exist) are for some, liberating maxims; for others they constitute paralyzing claims. What is the point of conducting research if no one except the researcher will see it to be of any value? How can we help to create civil society if there can be no agreement? How can one possibly argue for "moral leadership" (Furman & Shields, in press; Sergiovanni, 1992) or "moral purpose writ large" (Fullan, 2002) if everyone understands something different by these terms?

Some have claimed that this "post"-everything age is an era of relativism, in which each individual constructs his or her own reality—a reality that may bear little resemblance to any other, and which, in essence can never be shared or understood. This is the critique of David Harvey (2001) who complains, "obsessed with deconstructing and delegitimating every form of argument they encounter, they [post-modernists] can only end in condemning their own validity claims to the point where nothing remains for any reasoned basis of action" (p. 179).

Harvey (2001) goes on to make the important observation that the rhetoric of postmodernism "avoids confronting the realities of political economy and the circumstances of global power" (p. 179). The outcome, he suggests, is that "he who has the smoothest tongue or the raciest story has the power" (p. 180).

There is general agreement in most educational circles today that no research is free of bias (if interpreted as the researchers' perspectives and choices), that identifying the context and researchers' positionings is central to good research, and that research should address issues of power, hegemony, traditions, and hierarchies as well as quantifiable variables. None of this assuages Harvey's concern about the need for a basis for reasoned action. Indeed, his disquiet is still echoed today by researchers within and outside of the academy. What constitutes good research? Is it, in fact, a tightly constructed experimental design reported in the most highly regarded peer-refereed journals? Can we legitimately talk about the "worth" of our findings, or the "purpose" of the research, or are these concepts themselves outdated attempts to force post-modern wine into old functionalist bottles? Can we identify research that has a social purpose, that may be "useful" in some ways? What about research ethics and guidelines for ethical data collection, analysis, presentation, or representation? Have we learned anything in the intervening two millennia since Plato? How can we assess research findings that emerge from any of the "post" approaches and how can educational research speak to the messy complexity of educational leadership today?

LIVING WITH TENSIONS

Amid all of the rejection of absolutes and empirical truths, there is still a fundamentally important, but often overlooked awareness about relativism. Donmoyer (1985) recognized that "if empirical evidence is inadequate for judging the relative worth of interpretations, some other basis for assessing adequacy can and must be developed" (p. 13). We decry the potential dangers of accepting that all positions are intrinsically equal and that we cannot justify any differentiation among them; we live and act as though there is "truth," as though some bits of information are more intrinsically important or valuable than others, and as though we can "make a difference." Rorty (2001) elaborates this paradox:

> Relativism is the view that every belief on a certain topic, or perhaps about *any* topic, is as good as any other. No one holds this view. Except for the occasional cooperative freshman, one cannot find anybody who says that two incompatible opinions on a topic are equally good. The philosophers who get *called* "relativists" are those who say that the grounds for choosing between such opinions are less algorithmic than had been thought. . . . The real issue is not between people who think one view as good as another and people who do not. It is between those who think our culture, or purpose, or intuitions cannot be supported except conversationally, and people who still hope for other sorts of support. (p. 151)

Rorty's comment might seem to suggest that the post-modern perspectives are "straw men." Yet, this is not the case because relativistic viewpoints often influence theory, research, and public policy. He does, however, raise the question of what kinds of support we, as educational researchers may offer, for choosing among various positions, interpretations, and meanings.

Phillips and Burbules (2000) write that Dewey "gave us a clue" (p. 4) when he suggested that although some methods of inquiry are better than others, it does not follow "that the 'better' methods are ideally perfect. . . . we ascertain *how* and *why* certain means and agencies have provided warrantably assertible conclusions, while others have not and *cannot* do so" (p. 4). The question of what constitutes warrantably assertible conclusions remains to be addressed. Lyotard (2001), taking up a similar question, asks where legitimacy can reside (p. 167). Taking a simplified view of Habermas's notion of consensus, Lyotard rejects (as do I) the argument that obtaining consensus through discussion is a potential resolution. Consensus, he maintains, is obtained through the elimination of difference, through the subjugation of one perspective to another, or through the willing setting aside of one's belief in the supposed interests of the group. Lyotard (2001) says it persuasively: "Such consensus does violence to the heterogeneity of language games. And invention is always born of dissension" (p. 167).

Donmoyer (1985) did not suggest consensus as a way forward, but argued that: The work of Toulmin (1961, 1972, 1983), in particular, provides a theoretical basis for resolving the problem of relativism because he incorporates within his analysis the notion of purpose, a notion that reconstructed positivism cannot accommodate. (p. 18)

Thus, although the collective of "post" theories has not necessarily provided a satisfactory corrective to the difficulties and dangers of over-reliance on positivism, neither is the answer a return to large-scale scientific and empirical studies, with a concomitant wholesale rejection of other, more qualitative and subjective forms of research. In the next section of this chapter, I suggest that dialogue, understood in a Bakhtinian fashion, may help to provide a way forward.

A DIALOGICAL PARTICIPATORY ORIENTATION

Bakhtin's (1973) dialogic perspective may be useful here. His position is that there is no one "truth" or "certitude"; moreover, dialogue is not about deciding who is right or whose position is best. Instead, his concept of polyphony acknowledges that difference is at the base of human existence, and that a dialogical participatory orientation offers a way forward by generating new insights and understandings from that difference. He writes:

> Only a dialogical, participatory orientation takes the word of another person seriously and approaches it as a semantic position, as another point of view (p. 52) . . . These voices are not self-enclosed and are not deaf to one another. They constantly hear each other, call out to one another, and are mutually reflected in one another (especially in the microdialogs). Not a single essential action takes place, nor is a single essential thought expressed outside this dialog of "conflicting truths". . . . The concept of polyphony is incompatible with the representation of a single idea executed in the ordinary way. (pp. 62–63)

The "truth" is contained in the interaction and mutual reflection of all voices, interaction that has the potential for new and extraordinary insights, for understanding human existence and communication as essentially polyphonic and for learning to interact differently. Focusing on the particular purpose of the endeavor that brings us together, we avoid the temptation to seek consensus, but instead listen carefully, as we learn in and through a dialogue of conflicting truths. This is not a consensus approach. Likewise, Bakhtin himself is clear that it is not a relativistic approach, but one in which new meanings may be developed and shared. He adds that

> it is hardly necessary to mention that the polyphonic approach has nothing in common with relativism (nor with dogmatism). It should be noted that both relativism and dogmatism equally exclude all argumentation and all genuine dialog, either by making them unnecessary (relativism) or impossible (dogmatism). (p. 56)

Although Bakhtin's world is essentially one in which there are no absolutes, it certainly does not mean there are no realities. For Bakhtin, dialogue is ontological—we live dialogically, open to differences, to multiple voices (he calls it *heteroglossia*) and multiple perspectives. Moreover, he argues that it is in coming to grips with the Other, in coming into contact with interpretations that are different from our own that change occurs and new ideas are born. He writes:

> An idea does not *live* in one person's *isolated* individual consciousness—if it remains there it degenerates and dies. An idea begins to live, i.e., to take shape, to develop, to find and renew its verbal expression, and to give birth to new ideas only when it enters into genuine dialogical relationships with other, *foreign*, ideas. Human thought becomes genuine thought, i.e., an idea, only under the conditions of a living contact with another foreign thought, embodied in the voice of another person, that is, in the consciousness of another person as expressed in his word. (p. 71)

Relativism precludes dialogue in that, if there are no positions "more correct" or more worthwhile than any others, it is a waste of time to explore alternatives; alternatives become unnecessary. At the same time, dogmatism precludes the possibility for dialogue in that where there is no room for doubt, there is no room for change or growth. If one is so entrenched in his or her thinking that there is no possibility of other valid perspectives—other truths—then dialogue becomes not only unnecessary but impossible. On the other hand, if ideas come into being through contact with other "foreign" or different meanings, then dialogue becomes the basis, not only for life, but for research.

One could rephrase this reasoning to suggest that there is no one "more correct" or more worthwhile research methodology. Nevertheless, with Toulmin (as cited in Donmoyer, 1985), we might argue that some are better for specific purposes than others. A polyphonic dialogue about an educational research study, for example, investigating ways of teaching reading to non-English speaking children from homes of low socioeconomic backgrounds might include multiple approaches to several different questions, examined from various perspectives. A large-scale analysis of the correlation between reading achievement and socioeconomic status might best be done through a scientific quantitative approach. To understand the meaning of a particular strategy to a teacher and/or group of children, a researcher might select interviews or focus groups. A narrative, autobiographical study could explain how the teacher recognized his or her proclivity to blame the families and children of disadvantage for lower achievement, and how she had come to realize the need for new discursive self-positioning in order to "make a difference." A standpoint feminist approach within the larger question might reveal how educators can intervene most appropriately in the specific school context, taking account of their own standpoints as well as the circumstances of the students and their parents. The dialogue among the researchers involved, the inherent tensions and conflicts raised and debated, and the careful and respectful listening to one another might well achieve new, even "foreign" understandings that to date single research perspectives have failed to achieve.

Bakhtin as well as other thinkers—Buber (1970) and Friere (1970) for example—maintain that genuine dialogic interaction is relational; it grows out of a *participatory* approach to life. Buber (1970) asserts, for example, "In the beginning is the relation" (p. 69). We come to know, and to discern through relational encounters with the Other. Buber (1970) writes, "When we walk our way and encounter a man who comes toward us, walking his way, we know our way only and not his; for his comes to life for us only in the encounter" (p. 124). The concept is not unique to Buber; many others (see for example Freire, 1970; Margonis, 1992; Noddings, 1986; Palmer, 1998; Shields & Edwards, 2005; Sidorkin, 1999, 2002) assert the primacy of relationships and the absolute importance of understanding that relations rely on treating the other as a "Thou rather than an it" (Buber), as a Subject rather than an object (Freire)—treating the other, as Starratt (1991) framed it, "with absolute regard." Fromm puts it slightly differently. He differentiates between a *having* mode and a *being* mode. In the *being* mode, "We are what we express and enact in our relationships with others and the word. We do not *have* an ego and an identity based on it. Rather, we *be*, moment by moment, in the ways we affirm our specifically human nature" (as cited in Lankshear, 2003, p. 61).

Being in relationship to others, taking account of what Freire describes as "historically and culturally informed discourses" (as cited in Roberts, 2003, p. 174) offers a clue to a way forward in educational research. Freire argues that "there are no static unchanging truths that transcend time and space" but that "ideas must be understood contextually" (Roberts, 2003, p. 173). Being in participatory, dialogic relationship with another human being permits the inception of such an understanding. Context, as well as purpose, takes on renewed importance.

The notion of dialogical relations, of treating both relations and dialogue as ontological, as foundational to our way of life, is a starting point for getting beyond the certitude of logical, positivist scientific research as well as the relativistic "post" paradigms with their assertions that there is no knowable "truth." Inviting educational researchers to join in a dialogic, relational quest for understanding helps us to acknowledge, with Niels Bohr, that "the opposite of a true statement is a false statement, but the opposite of a profound truth can be another profound truth" (as cited in Palmer, 1998, p. 62).

For too long, educational researchers have failed to recognize the polyphonic nature of the endeavor. Regardless of our research paradigm, we have tried to argue for the "truth" and importance of our research findings, ignoring conflicting findings, taking no notice of purpose or context, often failing to seriously and dialogically engage with research from perspectives other than our own. Especially given the current return to a more pseudo-scientific research paradigm, this is an untenable position. We cannot afford either to ignore research coming from any single perspective as though it were somehow inherently flawed or, contrarily, to act as though it were the only tenable approach to research, for both stances deny the fundamental diversity and difference at the base of human existence. We cannot afford either relativism or dogmatism.

The postmodernist who maintains the impossibility of universal truths or indeed of any shared truths finds himself or herself still locked within a monological framework. Critical theorists advocate social justice, but sometimes argue that because a person comes from a well-known dominant position, he or she may have a less inherent right to speak. A standpoint feminist may argue vehemently for the right of a gay or lesbian woman to express her perspective, but close down comment by a member of the Christian right as inappropriate and hurtful. One way forward, I have argued is a turning away from monologism to Bakhtin's concept of dialogism, a concept that acknowledges that difference is at the base of human existence and learning.

WHAT DIFFERENCE DOES IT MAKE ANYWAY?

Why does any of this matter to the educational researcher setting out to build an academic career, or to investigate a burning issue related, perhaps, to improving literacy, or enhancing academic achievement, or ensuring social justice in schools? By way of response, let me share what was to me, an unsettling anecdote.

Not long ago, my department held a series of conversations to clarify what we mean by social justice. At one point, one of my colleagues asked Marie,[3] a senior colleague, what she would do, if during a class session, a Christian student stated categorically (and in the presence of a gay student) that homosexuality was wrong. The reply was, "I would permit the statement because everyone has the right to speak, but then would engage in a conversation to try to bring out other perspectives." Some other colleagues were outraged, "You would permit the statement!" they cried. "But it is hurtful; how long would you allow it?" Marie was stymied. She believed in listening to all voices, but felt both ridiculed and intimidated by her colleagues.

In reflecting on the painfully difficult situation, I would argue that Marie was coming from a well-developed postmodern perspective, but had failed to consider the basic challenge that might be proffered by colleagues who were firmly grounded in critical theory and the perspective of feminist standpoint theory and who therefore believed in the privileging of voices that had previously been marginalized and silenced. While Marie also wanted to hear from these neglected, perhaps even oppressed, voices, she asserted the fundamental right of all voices to be heard in the context of a classroom discussion.

Marie might have argued the need, as Giroux and McLaren have done, for a dialogue in which critical theory and postmodernism were integrated into "critical postmodernism" (as cited in Tierney, 1993, p. 28). Tierney elaborates by adding the concepts of agape and hope to "offer purpose and meaning" in a processual manner in which "individuals and groups engage one another to define what they mean by hope rather than accept the received wisdom of a community" (p. 28). This engagement was absent in the departmental conversation.

Further, Marie might have appealed to Bakhtin's (1973) suggestion "that one single voice is not capable of telling the truth. Only a multitude of simultaneous voices together may constitute the truth"(p. 156). She might, as Sidorkin (2002) would, have taken the argument even further. He argues that "a fully consistent message simply does not capture the complexity of moral life"; therefore, in a discussion in which certain perspectives are missing, one might go so far as to introduce them, because "the dialogical truth requires to have absent voice represented in some way" (1999, p. 66).

Sidorkin (2002) clarifies the problem, when talking about multiculturalism; he says that it "sits uneasily between two philosophical chairs, one of postmodernism and one of critical theory" (p. 173). The issue is that critical theorists (and many educational researchers and educational leaders) wanting to achieve more equitable, just, and caring learning environments, advocate concepts like justice and democracy, but fail to recognize the inherent contradictions between wanting these universal goods and the postmodern assertion that these concepts ultimately cannot be defined and are always relative. Coming down on one side or the other, they either permit all voices to be heard or deny previously privileged voices but have no way of moving forward, no way of making even tentative decisions about the relative merit of different positions. To move beyond these apparently irreconcilable positions, I believe it is first necessary to identify one's standpoint and its inherent assumptions and then to be willing to engage in dialogue with other, alternative epistemological stances.

A TEMPORARY RESTING PLACE[4]

My argument is that dialogue, understood ontologically in its most robust form, provides a way forward. It removes the necessity of epistemological battles and substitutes dialogic relations, new and dynamic understandings, and temporary conclusions. In order to engage the very political sphere of public education, educational researchers and educational leaders must act. We must accept what we determine to be the best insights available at a specific time for a unique context and an identified purpose, and live as if there were "truths," selecting some understandings, some approaches, and some goals as both desirable and ultimately achievable. We must take into consideration the importance of history and context, and as Giroux (2003) asserts, reject notions of education that are divorced from questions of power, place, ideology, and purpose (p. 152). Indeed, Giroux (2003) asserts that the analyses that are at the root of transformative pedagogy should be "both relational and contextual, as well as self-reflective and theoretical" (p. 158). Liston (2001) states that this would mean that in schools,

> Each student, teacher, or administrator would recognize that "in order for me to be me, I must engage in relationship with others, who must retain separate identities as they relate to me." . . . When we understand that our interactions with others enrich who we are, then we begin to seek out these interactions. (p. 209)

Dialogic relations may permit us to move forward toward better understanding, but they will not diminish the pluralism of our world. Palmer (1998) writes:

> Unlike the objectivist, I do not understand truth to be lodged in the conclusions we reach about objects of knowledge. How could it be, since the conclusions keep changing? I understand truth as the passionate and disciplined process of inquiry and dialogue itself, as the dynamic conversation of a community that keeps testing old conclusions and coming into new ones. (p. 104)

This redefinition of truth is a particularly important point. A school-based administrator, seeking to improve the reading ability of her students may not find "truth" sitting in her office examining the findings of various research studies. But she may discover a way forward, as she enjoins a dialogue with others in the school about the needs and characteristics of specific students, appropriate ways of assessing reading, about how to interpret the data from various testing programs, and about the meaning of a particular score or trend. Here, the dialogue may take as its starting point a question, a challenging situation, or even some data (believed by some to represent "truth"). The point is not to narrow the scope of how we make meaning, but to broaden it, relying on dialogic processes to understand and interpret data, even as we also rely on dialogic relationships to promote learning.

The conversations are not always easy, but they are necessary. Educational researchers cannot "put into the soul knowledge that isn't in it" (Plato, 1968, pp. 194–195). We can, however, engage in relational and dialogic participation with other researchers and with the world and work to which they are committed. From this engagement, we may develop new understandings that may help us to move forward, that may, for example, help to create just, equitable, and excellent schools for all children. We must persist in the inquiry but, with Bakhtin (1986), will always acknowledge that:

> There is neither a first nor a last word and there are no limits to the dialogic context (it extends into the boundless past and the boundless future). Even *past* meanings, that is, those born in the dialogue of past centuries, can never be stable (finalized, ended once and for all) — they will always change (be renewed) in the process of subsequent, future development of the dialogue. (p. 170)

The work, the new forms, our new understandings, may never be universal, never definitive, but they are critically important. It is therefore, the task of the educational researcher (and the educational leader) to ensure that the dialogue is unlimited and unending. Indeed, it is my hope and conviction that from this starting point we may once again move beyond the "new paradigm wars" and take educational research to a new level of meaning.

NOTES

1. The approach was worldwide, occurring in formal educational policies in New Zealand, Australia, Canada, and the United States during the last quarter of the nineteenth century.

2. For a discussion of the role of intelligence testing in the perpetuation of deficit thinking, see the excellent discussion in Valencia (1997).

3. The name is a pseudonym and the context has been modified enough to ensure confidentiality to participants.

4. The term comes from Wildavsky (1979), who posited several decades ago, that policy decisions were at best temporary resting places in that they might address one problem, but ultimately create the potential as they enter the already crowded and conflictual policy space, for new problems and challenges to emerge. The position holds, obviously for understandings that are always renewed, modified, altered in the continual dialogue that is life.

REFERENCES

Bakhtin, M. M. (1973). *Problems of Dostoevsky's poetics.* Ann Arbor, MI: Ardis.

Bakhtin, M. M. (1986). *Towards a methodology for the human sciences. Speech genres and other late essays* (V. McGee, Trans.). Austin, TX: University of Austin Press.

Bates, R. (1980). Educational administration, the sociology of science, and the management of knowledge. *Educational Administration Quarterly, 16*(2), 1–20.

Bishop, R., & T. Gymnn. (1999). *Culture counts: Changing power relations in education.* Palmerston North, NZ: Dunmore.

Boler, M. (2004). All speech is not free: The ethics of "affirmative action pedagogy." In M. Boler (Ed.), *Democratic dialogue in education: Troubling speech, disturbing silence* (pp. 3–14). New York: Peter Lang.

Buber, M. (1970). *I and thou* (W. Kaufmann, Trans.). New York: Charles Scribner's Sons.

Burbules, N. C. (1993). *Dialogue in teaching.* New York: Teachers College Press.

Burrell, G., & Morgan, G. (1979). *Sociological paradigms and sociological analysis.* London: Heinemann.

DeCastell, S. (2004). No speech is free: Affirmative action and the politics of give and take. In M. Boler (Ed.), *Democratic dialogue in education: Troubling speech, disturbing silence* (pp. 51–56). New York: Peter Lang.

Donmoyer, R. (1985). The rescue from relativism: Two failed attempts and an alternative strategy. *Educational Researcher, 14*(10), 13–20.

Donmoyer, R. (1999). The continuing quest for a knowledge base: 1976–1998. In J. Murphy & K. S. Louis (Eds.), *Handbook of research on educational administration* (2nd ed., pp. 25–44). San Francisco, CA: Jossey-Bass.

English, F. W. (2003). *The postmodern challenge to the theory and practice of educational administration.* Springfield, IL: Charles C. Thomas.

ESEA. (2002). Elementary and secondary education act. Retrieved March, 2004, from http://www.ed.gov/nclb/landing.jhtml.

Farella, J. (1993). *The wind in a jar.* Albuquerque: University of New Mexico Press.

Foucault, M. (2001). Power and knowledge. In S. Seidman & J. C. Alexander (Eds.), *The new social theory reader* (pp. 69–75). New York: Routledge.

Freire, P. (1970). *Pedagogy of the oppressed.* New York: Seabury Press.

Fullan, M. (2002). Moral purpose writ large. *The School Administrator, 8*(59), 14–16.

Furman, G. C., & Shields, C. M. (in press). Leadership for social justice and democratic community. In W.A. Firestone & C. Riehl (Eds.), *A new agenda: Directions for research on educational leadership*. New York: Teachers College Press.

Giroux, H. A., (2003). Pedagogy of the depressed: Beyond the new politics of cynicism. In M. L. Peters, C. Lankshear, & M. Olssen, M. (Eds.), *Critical theory and the human condition* (pp. 143–168). New York: Peter Lang.

Gould, S. J. (1981). *The mismeasure of man*. New York: W. W. Norton.

Greenfield, T. B. (1975). Theory about organization: A new perspective and its implications for schools. In M. Hughes (Ed.), *Administering education: International challenge* (pp. 71–99). Chicago, IL: The Midwest Center, University of Chicago.

Griffiths, M. (1998). *Educational research for social justice*. Philadelphia: Open University Press.

Hall, S. (2001). Cultural studies. In S. Seidman & J. C. Alexander (Eds.), *The new social theory reader* (pp. 88–100). New York: Routledge.

Harding, S. (1996). Rethinking standpoint epistemology: What is strong objectivity? In E. F. Keller & H. Longino (Eds.), *Feminism and science* (pp. 49–83). Oxford: Oxford University Press.

Harvey, D. (2001). The condition of postmodernity. In S. Seidman & J. C. Alexander (Eds.), *The new social theory reader* (pp. 176–183). New York: Routledge.

Herrnstein, R. J., & Murray, C. (1994). *The bell curve*. New York: Free Press.

Kuhn, T. S. (1970). *The structure of scientific revolutions* (2nd ed.). Chicago: University of Chicago Press.

Lankshear, C. (2003). On having and being: The humanism of Eric Fromm. In M. Peters, C. Lankshear, & M. Olssen (Eds.), *Critical theory and the human condition* (pp. 54–66). New York: Peter Lang.

Liston, D. D. (2001). *Joy as a metaphor of convergence*. Cresskill, NJ: Hampton.

Lyotard, J.-F. (2001). The postmodern condition. In S. Seidman & J. C. Alexander (Eds.), *The new social theory reader* (pp. 166–175). New York: Routledge.

Margonis, F. (1992). *New problems in child-centered pedagogy*. Philosophy of education yearbook.

Noddings, N. (1986). *Caring: A feminine approach to ethics and moral education*. Berkeley: University of California Press.

Palmer, P. J. (1998). *The courage to teach: Exploring the inner landscape of a teacher's life*. San Francisco, CA: Jossey-Bass.

Peters, M., Lankshear, C., & Olssen, M. (2003). Introduction. In M. Peters, C. Lankshear, & M. Olssen (Eds.), *Critical theory and the human condition* (pp. 1–14). New York: Peter Lang.

Philips, D. C., & Burbules, N. C. (2000). *Postpositivism and educational research*. New York: Rowman & Littlefield.

Plato. (1968). *The republic of Plato* (A. Bloom, Trans.). New York: Basic Books.

Roberts, P. (2003). Knowledge, dialogue, and humanization: Exploring Freire's philosophy. In M. L. Peters, C. Lankshear, & M. Olssen (Eds.), *Critical theory and the human condition* (pp. 169–183). New York: Peter Lang.

Rorty, R. (2001). Pragmatism, relativism, and irrationalism. In S. Seidman & J. C. Alexander (Eds.), *The new social theory reader* (pp. 147–155). New York: Routledge.

Seidman, S., & Alexander, J. C. (2001). Introduction. In S. Seidman & J. C. Alexander (Eds.), *The new social theory reader* (pp. 1–26). New York: Routledge.

Sergiovanni, T. J. (1992). *Moral leadership: Getting to the heart of schooling*. San Francisco, CA: Jossey-Bass.

Shields, C. M., & Edwards, M. M. (2005). *Dialogue is not just talk: A new ground for educational leadership*. New York: Peter Lang.

Sibicky, M. E. (1996). Understanding destructive obedience: The Milgram experiments. In P. S. Temes (Ed.), *Teaching leadership* (pp. 105–126). New York: Peter Lang.

Sidorkin, A. M. (1999). *Beyond Discourse: Education, the self, and dialogue*. Albny: State University of New York Press.

Sidorkin, A. M. (2002). *Learning relations*. New York: Peter Lang.

Smith, L. T. (1999). *Decolonizing methodologies*. Dunedin, NZ: University of Otago Press.

Starratt, R. J. (1991). Building an ethical school: A theory for practice in educational leadership. *Educational Administration Quarterly, 27*(2), 185–202.

Tierney, W. G. (1993). *Building communities of difference*. Toronto: OISE Press.

Valencia, R. R. (1997). *The evolution of deficit thinking*. Washington, DC: Falmer Press.

Wildavsky, A. B. (1979). *Speaking truth to power: The art and craft of policy analysis*. Boston: Little, Brown.

Willower, D. (1996). Inquiry in educational administration and the spirit of the times. *Educational Administration Quarterly, 32*(3), 244–365.

6

Standards for Research(er) Integrity in Educational Leadership: Implications for Current and Future Researchers

Michelle D. Young, University Council for Educational Administration; and Margaret Terry Orr, Bank Street College

In the 120 years since the founding of the Office of Education, a great deal of research has taken place in the field of education and part of that research has focused on the organization, management and leadership of schools. Recent federal initiatives, which include language about scientifically based research (SBR), reveal doubt in the quality of such research in education (Orr, Young, & Baker, 2006). Indeed, the notion of SBR, which can be found in several pieces of legislation including the federal No Child Left Behind (NCLB) legislation of 2001, the Reading Education Act of 1999, and the Education Sciences Reform Act of 2002, are examples of such skepticism.

The notion of SBR as well as the current focus on educational research in federal law has promoted significant debate in the educational research community. Such debate has centered on the purpose and nature of educational research, standards of quality in educational research, research methodology and epistemology, and the use of research in devising educational reforms. Of particular consequence have been the efforts of the National Research Council (NRC) to articulate the nature of scientific research in the field of education and to develop a set of principles for scientific educational research (Eisenhart & DeHann, 2005).

The primary purpose of this chapter is to contribute to a generative discussion taking place in this book as well as more broadly in the educational research field that focuses on the NRC's (2004) principles of research. Within this larger conversation, we make the case that having standards such as those provided by the NRC benefits the field of educational research.

However, we also draw the reader's attention to what is missing within the NRC standards, namely the issue of research integrity, as well as the need for broad interpretations of some elements of the standards.

The chapter begins with a brief discussion of national research standards that have been developed for education research and then reviews how such standards are communicated, practiced, and monitored within the field. We make the case that the field only loosely embraces and informally monitors the application of research standards, making it easy for questionable research to be distributed and used, usually to the detriment of our field. Subsequently we present our principles of research integrity, which center on the researcher's role in ensuring the validity or trustworthiness of research results (what we refer to in this article as researcher objectivity), making it easy for readers to assess the methods, analyses, and findings (what we have labeled transparency), and participating in a process that enables knowledgeable experts to provide thoughtful, timely and independent assessment of research objectivity and results (what we have referred to as scrutiny). We conclude with a discussion of implications for current practice and the preparation of future researchers in educational leadership.

STANDARDS FOR EDUCATIONAL RESEARCH

The first efforts of the federal government to establish a research component for education came with the passage of the Cooperative Research Act in 1954 (Getzels, 1978). Its development was quickly followed by criticism regarding the relevance of research to educational practice. Since that time, politicians and practitioners have wavered in their support for and or criticism of educational research. At the heart of current concerns, however, are issues of confidence—in the validity, accuracy, and generalizability of the findings and research methods used to yield the findings—and relevance. Exactly what has shaken confidence is difficult to determine, though conservative rhetoric, according to Shaker and Heilman (2004) has not helped. According to these scholars, negative conservative rhetoric has consistently raised questions about educational practice and the research on which that practice is based.

With regard to confidence, concerns have been raised as to whether educational research is rigorous and has definable research standards. It does, of course. In 1992, the American Educational Research Association (AERA), the leading community for educational researchers, delineated research norms and practices[1] for individuals and the field as a whole. This set of ethical research standards was then revised in 1996 and 2000 (AERA, 2005). The AERA standards address six areas and include: (a) the researchers' responsibilities to the field; (b) research populations, educational institutions, and the public; (c) intellectual ownership; (d) editing, reviewing, and appraising research; (e) sponsors, policymakers, and other use: and (f) students and student researchers (www.aera.net).

Also during the 1990s, the Commission on Educational Research (CER) reviewed the current state of education research and made recommendations. The commission addressed the state of education as a field, education research quality, and the field of educational research (Lagemann & Shulman, 1999). More recently, a consensus report created by sixteen researchers and a study director was published by the NRC (2002c) to influence congressional legislation on standards for educational research. Congressional legislation (HR-4875), which was released in 2000, contained a very restrictive definition of scientific research and included two sets of standards for quantitative and qualitative research. The NRC sponsored committee situated their much broader definition of scientific research in education (SRE) in "multiple theories," but also acknowledged that the definition "is also situated in politics, group dynamics, history, and context. To say it is a compromise(d) document is an understatement; to say it is not perfect is correct. To say it was not well-intentioned is inappropriate" (Eisenhart, 2005, p. 52).

Like AERA, the NRC proposed a clear set of standards, which can be used to guide the conduct of research and to evaluate the abuses of research. The standards include the following principles: (a) to pose significant questions that can be investigated empirically; (b) to link research to relevant theory; (c) to use methods that permit direct investigation of the question; (d) to provide an explicit and coherent chain of reasoning; (e) to replicate and generalize across studies; and (f) to make research public to encourage professional scrutiny and critique (NRC, 2002c).

In addition to providing guidance for legislation, the NRC also hoped to nurture the relationship between public trust in and investment in science and research institutions. As they clearly state: "The public will support science if it can trust the scientists and the institutions that conduct research." (2002c, p. 1). This requires that research institutions and the way in which these institutions conduct research be accountable for performing their work with integrity. What they found in their own review, however, was that while there are research standards, such as those provided by AERA, they are only loosely managed. The NRC further noted that the development of policies and procedures are necessary but not sufficient to ensure responsible conduct.

THE NEED FOR STANDARDS OF RESEARCH INTEGRITY

Because the quality and utility of research hinges in large measure on the skills and practices of individual researchers, it is essential that researchers ensure that their skills and practices are of unquestionable quality and impeccable integrity. The NRC standards, like those provided by AERA, when broadly interpreted, serve to benefit our field. As Tillman notes (in this volume), "the principles provide researchers with a framework that can be useful in deciding what is and is not important in the conceptualization, design, collection and analysis of specific types of research; and the principles may provide a template for those researchers whose research depends on tests, measurements, and inferences." However, like Tillman and Eisenhart (2005) we feel that a narrow definition of SBR as exclusively experimentalist is inappropriate for the field of education, and like Tillman and Eisenhart, we believe that the standards have utility beyond experimental design. However, we also believe that the standards do not go far enough with regard to one aspect of research. It is our position that, while there are many epistemological perspectives and methodological practices, there are certain principles of research integrity that all researchers should adhere to, particularly when research is used for or advocates educational policy or reform.

With regard to researcher ethics, the NRC did provide a set of principles for individual researchers. Through two separate inquiries, the NRC (2002a, 2002b) examined individual and institutional ethics in research and outlined principles for scientific inquiry in education. The NRC (2002a) defines research ethics as embodying "a commitment to intellectual honesty and personal responsibility for one's actions and to a range of practices that characterize the responsible conduct of research" (p. 5). These practices include: (a) intellectual honesty in proposing, conducting and reporting research; (b) accurately representing contributions in proposals and reports; (c) fairness in peer reviews; (d) collegiality in scientific interactions; (e) transparency in conflicts of interest; (f) protection of human subjects; (g) humane care of animals in research; and (h) adherence to the mutual responsibilities between investigators and their teams. In comparison to the general standards for research presented in the previous section, this set of ethical principles has received less attention and discussion by the educational research community. We would like to see this change.

At the same time that national efforts and debates have focused on promoting high quality and valid research, a spate of prominent policy significant research studies (e.g., Howell & Peterson, 2002; Levine, 2005; National Council on Teacher Quality, 2002; Stone, 2002) have been disseminated and used without peer review or objective media scrutiny. In fact, this "fugitive research," which has had a tremendous presence in the media and a strong impact on the policy community, disregards research standards, including standards for research integrity (Orr et al., 2006). Given a policy-making environment that prioritizes SBR to guide educational reform, one would expect that such obvious breaches of research standards would be challenged. The lack of significant challenge, creates serious dilemmas for the field of education, more serious than the dispersion of erroneous facts and findings. Addressing such dilemmas thoughtfully, objectively, and productively will require changes within the research community—changes that build on recent efforts to define principles and standards of research for education.

In any field, the quality of research depends primarily upon the "norms and practices of the community of researchers" (NRC, 2004, p. 22). The standards-compliance efforts of the research professions are limited. AERA (2005) officials, for example, explain that their standards are provided "to stimulate collegial debate and to evoke voluntary compliance by moral persuasion. . . . it is not the intention of the Association to monitor adherence to the Standards or to investigate allegations of violations to the Code" (p. 1). Thus, educational research norms and practices are passed on through two key practices: the training of novice educational researchers[2] and the review of juried research articles and peer-reviewed conference presentations (Orr et al., 2006).

These practices, while important, do not go far enough. First, the AERA research standards have not been formally adopted by the field of education.

Second, they are not explicitly incorporated into the textbooks used to train educational researchers. Third, there are no norms and processes to review independently released policy-relevant and controversial research, leaving it to individual scholars to respond, often with clouded speculation of their motivation. Fourth, current research standards do not emphasize the importance of researcher integrity.

Our definition of researcher integrity (Orr et al., 2006) relies on three principles that focus on how researchers handle and disseminate methodology and research findings, researcher objectivity, and research transparency and scrutiny.

Objectivity

Objectivity in research encompasses how research is conducted in an unbiased way in all phases of a research project, from design, through data collection, analysis and the development and dissemination of findings. Although traditional notions of objectivity, validity, and reliability have been thoroughly and appropriately challenged (viz., discussions and analyses contained within the three editions of Denzin and Lincoln's *Handbook of Qualitative Research* [2000, 2005]) by scholars operating out of various paradigmatic communities, each of these communities has ways to measure or assess whether or not research is of acceptable quality (Tillman, 2002).

In both quantitative and qualitative studies, research bias is often addressed through consideration of common internal and external validity threats and through the assessment of measurement reliability. Educational research methods textbooks commonly describe validity and reliability (though they may not use those terms), with a presumption that researchers want to develop unbiased results and will report findings fully and honestly (e.g., Creswell, 2005).

Cresswell (2005) explains that validity allows researchers to draw "meaningful and justifiable inferences" (p. 600) from their data. To achieve validity, a researcher must be able to produce an accurate account of measures, methods, analysis and interpretation. In developing this account, the author should strive for objectivity, rather than conforming the story to one's own wishes and prejudices, and she or he should not avoid discussing the possibility of error. Reliability, according to Cresswell

(2005) reflects the extent to which repeated measures using the same instrument are stable, consistent and free from measurement error. Critical here is laying bare the procedures followed in categorizing and linking data, the assumptions tested, and alternative explanations considered.

Of the six AERA (2005) research standards, Standard One—responsibilities to the field—specifically addresses the objective conduct of research. It details the researcher's responsibilities to conduct research in a rigorous and unbiased manner, as is appropriate to the research problem, methodology and study purpose. Accordingly, a researcher's responsibilities include: (a) conducting research without jeopardizing future research, the public standing of the field, or the discipline's research results; (b) not fabricating, falsifying, or misrepresenting authorship, evidence, data, findings, or conclusions; and (c) reporting findings to all relevant stakeholders, without selectively communicating their findings.

Additional standards, pulled from various sources, that are applicable here include: (a) address common internal and external threats to measurement and analytic validity, and do not extend generalization of findings beyond the group studied; (b) use qualitative data appropriately and do not substitute illustrative quotes for methodologically rigorous qualitative analysis; (c) demonstrate the reliability of measures and methods; (d) clearly raise and investigate alternative hypotheses; (e) build on existing theory and standards; (f) provide a coherent and explicit chain of reasoning, with attention paid to differences in definitions, methods, and results when combining multiple sources of data and studies into a coherent report; and (g) do not substitute ad hominem arguments for coherent data analysis (AERA, 2005; Cresswell, 2005; NRC, 2002a, 2002b; Orr et al., 2006).

A final, but very important, aspect of conducting research in an unbiased way involves revealing to the research consumer, the researcher's or funder's own value orientation and/or the existence of any conflict of interest. According to the NRC (2003), there are three types of conflict of interest—scientific, ethical, and financial—particularly in the review of protocols. The council's examination of conflict of interest focused primarily on ensuring participant protection, but found other areas in which conflict of interest may exist. For example, there should be rigorous scientific and ethical review of research protocols, particularly to ensure that financial and other interests do not "distort the conduct of research with human subjects" (NRC, 2003, p. 10).

Transparency

In addition to conducting research in an objective manner, researchers must make their methodological choices and analytic actions clear for other scholars to review, replicate and understand how findings were reached and conclusions drawn (Orr et al., 2006). The primary criterion underlying this principle is to be fair, unbiased, and responsible in reporting research as one is in conducting research.

The NRC (2003) argued for transparency and openness in the research process, particularly among those most likely to be harmed—research subjects. According to the NRC, research should be sufficiently transparent and accessible so "those who stand to benefit or be harmed by the research should have an opportunity to comment on the research design and operation, to participate in the research, and to have access to study findings" (NRC, 2003, p. 14).

This transparency principle is also reflected in AERA's (2005) research Standard One, which outlines the researcher's responsibility to be transparent about how the research was conducted, how the findings were reached, and what the boundaries for generalizability were. These responsibilities include reporting research conceptions, procedures, results, and analyses accurately and in sufficient detail so that knowledgeable, trained researchers can understand and interpret them and to report findings to the public in a way that straightforwardly communicates the practical significance for policy, including limits in effectiveness and in generalizability to situations, problems, and contexts, taking care not to misrepresent the practical or policy implications of their research or the research of others (www.aera.net).

Scrutiny

The primary mechanism used by the research field to facilitate high quality, objective and unbiased research and to protect the field from misuse of poor research is external, and usually blind, peer review (Orr et al., 2006). Lagemann and Shulman (1999) describe peer review as a helpful tool for verifying not only the reliability of research but also its educational importance prior to its publication. Given that policy-relevant research often yields controversial findings or competing findings among even thoughtfully done studies, Shulman (2005) stresses objectivity in the conduct of research, transparency about conflicts of interest, and the standard use of a peer review process.

A trend has emerged, however, in which controversial and policy-relevant but "premature" research findings are submitted to the public without peer review (Cibulka, as cited in Viadero, 2005). Two common reasons given by researchers who eschew peer review are the improved timeliness of press releases over peer-reviewed journals and the desire to influence policy making. In an article criticizing university research that is released without peer review, Viadero (2005) noted: "It's a refrain that has become common lately as research on hot-button issues move directly from the author's computer printer to a press release" (p. 1). Although the peer review process has its limitations, it does have its strengths (e.g., identify inappropriate analysis, overgeneralization of data, and alternative explanations, etc.), and it is essential for the credibility of research in the field of education (Finn, 2002; Lagemann & Shulman, 1999).

In an effort to identify effective practice in peer review, Shulman (2005) recommends the following to reviewers: (a) address how well the study design and analysis permit the claims being made for the interpretation of the data; (b) identify other studies that complement or contradict the findings and how these results compare; and (c) consider how reasonable are the policy-relevant claims made by the authors based on the evidence in the study. Given the potential impact that policy-relevant research can have on children, schools, and educational resources, it is essential that such research undergo scrutiny through a high quality, independent peer review process before being released to the public.

IMPLICATIONS FOR THE PRACTICE OF EDUCATIONAL RESEARCHERS AND THE PREPARATION OF FUTURE LEADERSHIP SCHOLARS

The standards for researcher integrity that we have outlined above set clear expectations for researchers regarding their responsibilities to ensure objectivity, transparency, and scrutiny in their work. However, as the NRC points out, merely having research standards is not enough. There must be widespread acceptance, formal adoption, and, most important, consistent use.

Although some scholars may refuse to accept the standards suggested by the NRC (2002c), AERA (2005), and those we have suggested for researcher integrity, we believe that many others will agree that they are both needed and useful. A continued dialogue concerning their interpretation and use would likely lead to even greater understanding, possible adaptation and acceptance.

Once in use, however, we may find that "fugitive studies" continue to be released. It is for this reason that we feel it necessary to suggest to our national professional organizations, like AERA, that an independent research review board (or more than one) be established. The review board would have as its primary purpose the review of policy-relevant research released to the public without peer review. A review board of this nature could help to ensure that even researchers who disregard elements of widely accepted research standards are held accountable.

In addition to formal adoptions of standards for research and researcher integrity and the establishment of an independent review board, we also believe it is necessary that the training of future educational researchers be carefully evaluated and, if needed, reconstructed.

In a recent Educational Researcher article, Eisenhart and DeHann (2005) argue that a "fundamental component of training programs that prepare scientifically based educational researchers is socialization into the norms of scientific inquiry" (p. 5). The norms they speak of are captured by the AERA, NRC and researcher integrity principles described in this chapter, and like Eisenhart and DeHann, we do not think that educational leadership programs currently ensure such socialization.

In fact, in educational leadership programs the tendency for many years has been the collapsing of Ph.D. and Ed.D. programs and thus the dilution of research training in an attempt to make "one size fit all." Although there are certainly advantages to training future researchers and practitioners together, there are also disadvantages. Scholars in many fields have discussed the merits of separate programs over the years (see Eisenhart & DeHann, 2005; Council of Graduate Schools, 1966; Sarason, 1993). In order to ensure that future researchers are well prepared to contribute to the knowledge base in education, we believe that educational leadership departments should separate the two programs, providing well-designed Ed.D. programs that prepare educational professionals and Ph.D. programs that prepare researchers.

Within these Ph.D. programs, Eisenhart and DeHann (2005) assert that educational researchers need training in five areas: (a) diverse epistemological perspectives, (b) diverse methodological strategies, (c) varied contexts of educational practice, (d) the principles of scientific inquiry, and (e) an interdisciplinary focus (p. 7). We would add to this list training and socialization in both content and theory appropriate to their area of study as well as principles of research integrity. As burgeoning scholars, it must be made clear that participation within a community of research entails a serious responsibility to ensure objectivity, transparency, and scrutiny — the essence of researcher integrity.

CONCLUSION

Extending the discussion on the NRC standards for scientific education research, we have argued for the adoption of standards for researcher integrity that tend to the importance of objectivity, transparency and scrutiny. We have also argued, however, that in order for any research standards to make a difference they must become normative, through official adoption by the field and the training of and socialization of future educational researchers. We have suggested that current models of informal agreement and graduate research training are inadequate to support norms of rigor and integrity in research and we have made a number of recommendations for addressing these problems, including the development of an independent research review board.

The continual improvement of educational opportunities for all children depends upon advancing the knowledgebase in our field. As we continue discussions focused on research methods, modes of inquiry, ways on knowing, and standards for research and research integrity, we must use these discussions to strengthen our professional communities of inquiry. "The practice of researchers with diverse perspectives tangling with the warrants and claims of inquiry has traditionally served to transform knowledge and understanding within any field" (Young, 2001, p. 5). The generative, reflexive and critical discussions of today hold great promise for building a strong sense of responsibility and integrity among the researchers of today and tomorrow, from which the field will certainly benefit.

NOTES

1. While we acknowledge that the AERA and NRC research standards may not find acceptance among all educational researchers, they do represent beliefs about research quality and integrity for the majority of researchers in the field.

2. Unfortunately, educational research textbooks are typically silent on the topic of research integrity, providing little guidance on researcher responsibility to ensure research rigor, as demonstrated by a review of educational research text books for their coverage of researcher conduct and integrity issues (Creswell, 2005; Denzin & Lincoln, 2005).

REFERENCES

American Educational Research Association. (2005). *Ethical standards*. Retrieved June 7, 2005, from http://aera.net/aboutaera/?id=222.

Council of Graduate Schools in the United States. (1966). *The doctor's degree in professional fields*. Washington, DC: Association of Graduate Schools and the Council of Graduate Schools in the United States.

Creswell, J. W. (2005). *Educational research: Planning, conducting, and evaluating quantitative and qualitative research* (2nd ed.). Upper Saddle River, NJ: Merrill.

Denzin, N., & Lincoln, Y. (Eds.). (2000). *Handbook of qualitative research* (2nd ed.). Thousand Oaks, CA: Sage.

Denzin, N., & Lincoln, Y. (Eds.). (2005). *Handbook of qualitative research* (3rd ed.). Thousand Oaks, CA: Sage.

Eisenhart, M. (2005). Science plus: A response to the responses to *Scientific Research in Education*. *Teachers College Record, 107*(1), 52–58.

Eisenhart, M., & DeHann, R. L. (2005). Doctoral preparation of scientifically based education researchers. *Educational Researcher, 34*(4), 3–13.

Finn, C. (2002). The limits of peer review. *Education Week, 21*(34), 30, 34.

Getzels, J. W. (1978). Paradigm and practice: On the impact of basic research in education. In P. Suppes (Ed.), *Impact of research on education: Some case studies* (pp. 477–522). Washington, DC: National Academy of Education.

Howell, W., & Peterson, P. (2002). *The education gap: Vouchers and urban schools*. Washington, DC: Brookings Institution Press.

Lagemann, E. C., & Shulman, L. S. (1999). Introduction. The improvement of education research: A complex quest. In E. C. Lagemann and L. S. Shulman (Eds.), *Issues in education research, problems and possibilities* (pp. 309–330). San Francisco, CA: Jossey-Bass.

Levine, A. (2005). *Educating school leaders*. The Education Schools Project. Retrieved April 30, 2005, from http://www.edschools.org/pdf/Final313.pdf.

National Research Council. (2002a). *Integrity in scientific research: Creating an environment that promotes responsible conduct*. Institute of Medicine. Washington, DC: National Academies Press.

National Research Council. (2002b). *Responsible research: A systems approach to protecting research participants*. Center for Education, Division of Behavioral and Social Sciences and Education. Washington, DC: National Academies Press.

National Research Council (NRC) Committee of Scientific Principles for Education Research. (2002c). *Scientific research in education*. R. J. Shavelson & L. Towne (Eds.). Washington, DC: National Academies Press.

National Research Council (NRC) (2003). *Responsible research: A system approach to protecting research participants*. Washington, DC: National Academies Press.

National Research Council. (2004). *Advancing scientific research in education*. Washington, DC: National Academies Press.

National Council on Teacher Quality. (2002). *Teacher Quality Report*. Washington, DC: Author.

Orr, M. T., Young, M. D., & Baker, B. (2006). *Researcher integrity: Direct and indirect fallout in the field*. Manuscript submitted for publication.

Sarason, S. B. (1993). *The case for change: Rethinking the preparation of educators*. San Francisco, CA: Jossey-Bass.

Shaker, P., & Heilman, E. E. (2004, July). The new common sense of education: Advocacy research versus academic authority. *Teachers College Record, 106*(7), 1444–1470.

Shulman, L. S. (2005). Seek simplicity . . . and distrust it. Commentary. *Education Week, 24*(39), 36, 48.

Stone, J. E. (2002). *The value-added gains of NBPTS-certified teachers in Tennessee: A brief report*. Retrieved June 1, 2005, from http:///www.educationconsumers.com.

Tillman, L. (2002). Culturally sensitive research approaches: An African American perspective. *Educational Researcher 31*(9), 4–12.

Viadero, D. (2005, May 18). Release of unreviewed studies sparks debate. *Education Week*. Retrieved June 1, 2005, from http://www.edweek.org/articles/2005/05/18/37peer/h24/html?ral.

Young, L. J. (2001). Border crossings and other journeys: Re-envisioning the doctoral preparation of educational researchers. *Educational Researcher, 30*(5), 3–5.

7

Research on Educational Leadership: Knowledge We Need for the World We Live In

Carolyn Riehl, Columbia University

Anticipating what lies ahead for research and knowledge in the field of educational leadership can be a daunting task. With the ink barely dry on the calendar pages for an already tumultuous new century, one wonders what the future will require of its educational leaders—whether the challenges to come will match in any way those of the past. Will schools resemble the current familiar model, or will technology, privatization, and other forces alter their fundamental character? Will the body of knowledge about schooling and leadership gleaned from the last 150 years, since the early research of Ellwood Cubberley and Horace Mann, be of any use at all to those attempting to manage, much less invent, schools of the future? Should new research help leaders recapitulate modernity's quest for rationality, certainty, and the hope for progress, or should it help them learn to live more comfortably with randomness, unsolvable dilemmas, and the interplay of spirit, body, and mind? What will be the metrics by which we measure the value of any form of knowledge as a guide for educational leaders? In a culture where the distinctions between fact and fiction, or science and belief, are blurred, is one source of understanding more authoritative than another?

In this essay, I offer some reflections on the current moment in educational leadership research. I write not from a vantage point of exceptional expertise in the philosophy of science or in research methodology, but instead as a researcher keenly interested in the whys and hows of our collective enterprise. With a background in the humanities and the social sciences, with experience in both quantitative and qualitative research, and with epistemological inclinations that roam among several options, I juggle many of the tensions and ambiguities experienced by others in our field. I consider any criticisms and suggestions I offer here to apply first of all to myself.

THE QUEST FOR SCIENTIFIC
RESEARCH . . . AND OTHER KNOWLEDGE WE NEED

Consider the following scenario: a high school principal anticipates the process of assigning students to courses for the next academic year. She ponders the school's current policy of separating students into AP, honors, general, and business levels of mathematics. She has seen articles claiming that students' chances of college acceptance increase if they take the most advanced courses their high schools offer, and she knows that the local superintendent is intent on raising the number of students who take AP classes. But she has read that failure rates rise—at least initially—when all students are placed in highly challenging courses and that some watered-down courses are "honors" in name only. She has read the research indicating that lower-ability students do better in mixed-ability classrooms, but wonders if that's fair to all students. She has talked to her school's "elite parents" who utilize a variety of pressures to make sure their children have the best teachers and classmates who don't hold them back. She has talked with teachers who seem dismayed by the effort it takes to differentiate instruction in mixed-ability classes. She has even read Roddy Doyle's (1996) novel *The Woman Who Walked into Doors*, and winced at its narrator's emotionally compelling—though fictional—account of what it was like in the back of the classroom of her low track class. Barraged with all of this information, how can she assess what counts as durable knowledge to guide her leadership? And, for those of us who want to support her efforts, how should we develop knowledge she can use?

In an environment with many complex and contested sources of information and with many disparate interests at work, it seems understandable that efforts might be made to simplify the search for authoritative knowledge to guide policy and practice. That is one way to interpret recent actions of the U.S. federal government. Over fifteen years ago, Chester

Finn, then Assistant Secretary at the Department of Education, wrote that the labors of educational researchers "haven't produced enough findings that Americans can use or even see the use of" (1988, p. 5). Acting on this sort of long-standing frustration about the quality of educational research, the government has used several major initiatives as platforms for pressing for "evidence-based scientific research" to guide educational practice. In the words of several key players in this unfolding drama, "the American people through their elected leaders are (again) manifesting their faith in science as a force for improved public policy" (Feuer, Towne, & Shavelson, 2002, p. 4).

Several examples of these initiatives come to mind. In 1997, the federal government convened the National Reading Panel to summarize knowledge on effective strategies for teaching children to read (National Institute of Child Health and Development, 2000). The Panel chose to review only research that was experimental or quasi-experimental in design, research in which a clear instructional strategy was being tested with a sample considered large enough to be useful. The Panel acknowledged that only a small portion of the research corpus on reading met these standards for review, thereby frustrating not a few members of that research community.

In 2002, the U.S. Department of Education's Institute of Education Sciences established the What Works Clearinghouse to review research evidence on effective instructional strategies in many curricular domains. Like the Reading Panel, the Clearinghouse has focused on "scientifically-based research," which it defines as research that draws on observation or experiment and makes causal claims only from random-assignment experiments or other designs that can test alternative explanations for results (What Works Clearinghouse, 2004). Finally, the No Child Left Behind legislation, which ostensibly has sought to promote equity and excellence in achievement for all students, also puts a high value on evidence-based practice and scientifically based research in the programs it mandates and funds, citing the latter term over one hundred times in the law (U.S. Congress, 2001).

Through these initiatives, the federal government seems intent on focusing the attention of the educational community on particular forms of research that can provide convincing evidence for the most efficient and effective ways of generating desired outcomes. The assumption seems to be that if effective educational strategies can be specified through research, it will be a relatively straightforward matter for practitioners to adopt and use these practices.

This effort has not been met with uncritical acceptance from the research community. Many scholars feel that the federal government has promoted a too-narrow definition of scientific research, has selectively ignored good research that contradicts its policy initiatives, and has allowed itself to be swayed by its political and ideological goals (e.g., Allington, 2002; Erickson, 2005; Erickson & Gutierrez, 2002; Yatvin, Weaver, & Garan, 2003). Given these assessments, it is hard to ascribe fully benevolent intentions to the government. Nonetheless, many thoughtful observers would agree that attention indeed should be focused on improving the quality of research in education and articulating more clearly what counts as authoritative knowledge for the field (Eisenhart, 2005). In that respect, at least, the federal government's efforts have had an impact, by moving the conversation about research to a new level of visibility and intensity.

In 2000, the federal government invited the National Research Council (NRC), an arm of the relatively independent National Academies, to get into the fray by providing counsel on how to define and conduct scientific research in education (Eisenhart & Towne, 2003; Moss, 2005). The task force report, *Scientific Research in Education* (NRC, 2002), has garnered unprecedented attention and generated much debate, not only because it has sometimes been equated with the federal perspective (an interpretation its authors and others refute), but because it raises many provocative issues on its own terms.

The NRC report takes off from the premise that we do need scientific research in education and seeks to clarify what that research ought to be like. The report asserts that scientific inquiry in education is no different from scientific inquiry in other fields, portraying it as "a continual process of rigorous reasoning supported by a dynamic interplay among methods, theories, and findings" (NRC, 2002, p. 2). The report articulates six general principles for this form of research. These principles, in essence, should serve as norms and habits that can help a community create and self-monitor a "culture of scientific inquiry" (Feuer, Towne, & Shavelson, 2002). The six principles are:

1. Pose significant questions that can be investigated empirically;
2. Link research to relevant theory;

3. Use methods that permit direct investigation of the question;
4. Provide a coherent and explicit chain of reasoning;
5. Replicate and generalize across studies; and
6. Disclose research to encourage professional scrutiny and critique.

There is more nuance in the NRC report than in the federal government's approach to scientific research. For example, while both perspectives emphasize the importance of research based on strong evidence, the report does not focus exclusively on the empirical investigation of objective, measurable phenomena, the original hallmark of empirical social science (Bernstein, 1976). Instead, the NRC report suggests that some phenomena of interest to educational researchers must be studied by tapping human agents' own "understanding, intentions, and values as well as their observable behavior" (NRC, 2002, p. 16). The report also eschews causal determinism, another traditional defining feature of empirical science. Instead, the report expresses an understanding that human actions are not the inevitable (or even probabilistic) result of determinate factors, but rather are enacted as meaningful choices and voluntary actions of human agents, along with their "unintended or aggregate consequences" (p. 15). Thus, in the view of one of its authors, the report "can accommodate the role of both patterned behavior and human intentionality in human activity" (Eisenhart, 2005, p. 53).

While the federal government's approach seems to assume a linear process by which authoritative research is translated into indelible guides for practice, the NRC (2002) report challenges this notion. Moreover, the report eschews investing scientific research with exclusive authority and acknowledges that insights from other forms of knowledge, such as the humanities, can also help guide educational practice.

Despite these positive features, the NRC report has garnered substantial criticism. For example, Maxwell (2004) argues that the report seems to emphasize the study of associations between discrete variables that have been abstracted from the contexts in which they occur, rather than a more holistic process-oriented approach toward lived experience. Gee (2005) finds the six guiding principles of the report to be overly vague and thus potentially confusing and even dangerous. Many respondents seem to feel that the report pays far too little attention to the knowledge-building purposes that qualitative research can serve best (e.g., Erickson, 2005;

Moss, 2005). Eisenhart (2005), a co-author of the report with strong credentials in qualitative research, agrees that the report could have emphasized qualitative research more and also suggests that it could have gone farther in acknowledging "the infeasibility and absurdity of experimental and quasi-experimental research for most research questions in educational research" (p. 56). Walker (2005) suggests that the report pays insufficient attention to critical issues such as the role of the researcher in the research process and insidious patterns by which different research topics and strategies are privileged or silenced. Erickson and Gutierrez (2002) take issue with the assumption that educational treatments could be considered "relatively replicable entities like chemical compounds or surgical procedures or hybrid seed corn" (p. 21). Such an approach, they argue, is not science but scientism, or the idealization of science. Moreover, it ignores much of what we know about how real scientists really work.

Criticisms such as these may be valid. Nonetheless, the report does advance several tenable assertions, such as the following:

1. scientific research is research that relies on the careful empirical examination and analytic interpretation of evidence;
2. scientific research is one very useful form of knowledge-generating activity, but not the only form;
3. scientific research can be used to investigate important questions about a variety of phenonema;
4. scientific research can explicate both how and why things happen; and
5. scientific research can and should be held accountable for conforming to standards for design, evidence, reasoning, and public visibility.

The field of educational leadership research can locate much of value in the report. Our field, like other subfields in education, may reject the suggestion, advanced by the federal government and echoed to some degree in the NRC report, that experimental designs ought to be the preferred research method of choice. Still, it may not be a bad thing to be expected to justify the research designs and methodologies we use and to consider more seriously the use of designs and methods that can meet the standards raised in the NRC report.

Nonetheless, the NRC report seems to have touched a raw nerve within the research community, including the field of educational leadership. The agitation it has stirred up seems fundamentally to be a concern over the definition and privileged status of "science." On the one hand, people seem to resent particular definitions of science, taking issue with narrow specifications of the proper objects of scientific study, the role of values in scientific inquiry, or the positioning of the researcher vis-à-vis the research. On the other hand, there is resentment over the dominance of science and how it has accrued material and symbolic attention, status, and tangible resources and benefits that are denied to other forms of knowledge.

An emphasis on science is, of course, the hallmark and legacy of modernity. As many historians of science have pointed out, the model of empirical-theoretical inquiry that was developed from Enlightenment traditions of objectivity and rationality was initially seen as a positive innovation. Scientific knowledge was a trustworthy improvement upon knowledge derived through superstition, tradition, authority, or mere logic (Kerlinger, 1964). As Bernstein (1976) expresses about empirical inquiry:

> There are great virtues in these traditions which cannot be lightly dismissed. At their best, they have insisted upon clarity and rigor. They have been committed to the ideal of public and intersubjective tests and criticisms in which any knowledge claim is recognized as fallible and subject to further inquiry. There has been a healthy skepticism toward unbridled speculation and murky obscurantist thought. (p. xxii)

To avoid the twin dangers of being swayed by ideology or enamored of mere facts, the scientific tradition incorporated the ideal of the disinterested observer who describes, explains, or interprets but does not interfere with the apprehension of objective truth. The aim of this approach was "to resolve differences of opinion about matters of fact through the use of procedures whose validity does not depend upon the prejudices of the user" (Cohen, 1989, p. 7). Initially, this implied the need for a completely neutral, almost invisible and interchangeable, observer. Over time, however, this notion was altered. As Cohen (1989) notes:

> the norm of intersubjective testability requires that scientists be on constant alert for sources of bias and that they make every effort to develop

procedures for the elimination of bias once it is identified. This norm constitutes a reformulation of the older notion of scientific knowledge as objective. Few scientists today would claim that their knowledge is objective—in the sense that it corresponds to reality and is independent of the knower. (p. 62)

Scientific inquiry was intended to be a neutral and therefore trustworthy activity, but it was not expected to be uninterested in the real world. Initially, at least, objective empirical knowledge—that is, science—was thought to have moral and political virtues in addition to intellectual ones, and it would permit humans to engage in "enlightened action" (Bernstein, 1976, p. xxiii).

In short, the origins of science can be seen as salutary developments in the history of human thought. However, as Bernstein (1976) comments, the ascendancy of scientific thinking seems to have resulted in a trajectory with "ever more severe restriction on what counts as genuine knowledge and on limits of rational argument" (p. xxiii). In education, the current emphasis on evidence-based knowledge is viewed by many as an alarming node on this pathway.

But other countervailing forces have sought to keep broadening the definition of genuine knowledge, in part by modifying our understandings of science itself. Kuhn's (1970) explication of the theory-laden nature of scientific inquiry debunked the idea that science is purely objective. Feminist epistemologies and other standpoint-based theories (e.g., Collins, 2000; Lather, 1991) have further challenged the notion of the disinterested, neutral observer and have offered new perspectives on the role of values in research as well as the researcher's own social location. The tradition of critical-hermeneutic inquiry, first advanced by the Frankfurt School and later expanded through the work of phenomenologists, symbolic interactionists, and others in the interpretive tradition, has provided important impetus for this work.

These are valid and useful correctives. But I believe that they do not obviate a fundamental characteristic of science, which is the emphasis on clearly laid out evidence, interpreted via concepts and theories that can have applicability beyond the particular context and phenomena being studied. What distinguishes science is not just the checks and balances provided by objectivity, leaving personal beliefs, perceptions, biases, values, attitudes, and emotions out of it, but "because science ultimately appeals to evidence: propositions are subjected to empirical test" (Kerlinger, 1964, p. 8).

If the essence of science is its reliance on evidence, then even the most radical kind of inquiry, with a "positioned" researcher studying the subjective understandings of a research participant, with little interest in generalization, could be held to the standard of careful evidence, carefully interpreted. But espousing this core understanding of science—as evidence scrupulously gathered, interpreted, and made available for public scrutiny—does exclude some knowledge-building efforts from the scientific canopy. This still irritates some, and people continue to insist that the definition of science could be expanded. For example, Erickson (2005) suggests that a big tent approach to science could be justified by hearkening back to a medieval understanding of science as "careful thinking accountable to public expert criticism" (p. 5). This approach would incorporate non-empirical enterprises like normative theory and philosophy as science, consistent with the medieval view of theology as the "queen of science."

Another strategy would be to maintain a relatively narrow definition of "science" and instead broaden the definition of "useful knowledge" to include more than science. Shavelson (2002) quotes Lee Cronbach, one of the most eminent quantitative methodologists of the twentieth century, as saying:

> The special task of the social scientist in each generation is to pin down the contemporary facts. Beyond that, he shares with the humanistic scholar and the artist in the effort to gain insight into contemporary relationships, and to align the culture's view of man [sic] with present realities. To know man as he is is no mean aspiration. (p. 126)

Cohen (1989) notes that "scientific knowledge is not coextensive with all human knowledge" and suggested that perhaps science has attracted more critics because of "the failure of the worshipers of science to recognize and acknowledge the limitations of scientific knowledge" (p. 4). This is essentially what Bernstein (1976) calls for with the restructuring of social and political theory. In his view, the "social disciplines" are considered sciences because they were built from empirical theory as contrasted with empiricism or normative theory. Finessing the question of just what counts as science, Bernstein argues that these disciplines should be "empirical, interpretative, and critical" (p. xx). In so doing, he creates an inclusive vision of a social discipline that incorporates more than its scientific dimensions.

A useful perspective is presented by Burkhardt and Schoenfeld (2003), who distinguish among three approaches to research: humanities, science, and engineering. The humanities approach involves scholarly reflection and the production of new ideas and insights, often in the form of critical commentary. Research in this vein does not depend upon empirical evidence. This permits the free rein of innovation and creative thought, subject to values of scholarship such as plausibility, consistency, or fidelity to the referenced work of others. But the lack of empirical support is, as Burkhardt and Schoenfeld note, a "profound weakness," and it often seems to reach forward to an "evidence-based" approach to knowledge development—that is, to science. Science, in turn, while generating assertions based both on logical arguments and evidence, does not by itself produce practical solutions. The engineering approach seeks not only to explicate how the world works but also to help it work better. Drawing on knowledge from science and humanities, work in the engineering approach is intended to design, test, and evaluate practical products such as tools, materials, or processes. Any given research effort might combine two or three of these approaches; in fact, as Stokes (1997) argues, theoretical knowledge development (the goal of "science") might proceed most effectively when practical, engineering problems are also addressed.

In short, it could easily be argued that science is only one kind of research needed in a robust domain of knowledge and scholarship, and it might be more helpful to knock science off its privileged pedestal than to draw a wider cloak around what counts as science.

It is worth noting that other fields are also preoccupied with efforts to reposition scientific knowledge within their respective knowledge domains. For example, the U.S. medical community, in recent years, has placed a great deal of emphasis on "evidence-based practice" and has sought to develop standards for the production and use of knowledge about medical care that has strong warrants by virtue of research strategies such as double blind randomization (e.g., Drazen, 2003; Schoenfeld & Scheiman, 2003). In contrast, the business community's stance toward scientific knowledge has been challenged as having too little to do with practice and too likely to lead to the preparation of business leaders who have little visceral understanding of the real enterprises they will soon manage (Bennis & O'Toole, 2005).

Debates about what counts as science and what counts as authoritative knowledge are interesting, and they have real purchase in the current funding and regulatory environment in education. For example, Mayer (2000) argues that educational research should be conducted within the boundaries of the scientific tradition in order to maintain a valued reputation as a scientific enterprise. But these debates are not the most important issues for researchers to worry about. Instead, we could focus on generating whatever kinds of knowledge it takes to improve practice. The NRC report suggests, albeit in subtle ways, that scientific research holds special weight as a form of knowledge, but that other forms of knowledge are also essential. I believe this is a formulation the educational leadership community can live with, and it would be more productive to accept the definitions it establishes and work to improve all forms of knowledge, rather than to strain against the definitions.

UNDERSTANDINGS THAT
SHAPE KNOWLEDGE ABOUT LEADERSHIP

If we could move into a more productive discussion about how best to develop all forms of knowledge—accepting boundaries among different forms of scholarship and not worrying too much about what counts as "science," perhaps both our knowledge base and those who use it would benefit. As we move in this direction, however, it may be useful to consider several key ideas that have begun to influence how we think about leadership and therefore how we might revise our strategies for conducting research.

Leadership as a Situated Social Practice

Researchers have sometimes sought to identify leadership qualities, styles, or skills that will lead to specific organizational or educational outcomes. This may be a misguided quest. Leadership usually occurs within complex social systems, whether they are small groups or large organizations. As von Bertalanffy (1968) articulates in his original work on general systems theory, multiple nondeterminate pathways within a system can produce the same outcomes, a phenomenon he termed equifinality. Erickson and Gutierrez (2002) make a similar point in challenging Hume's "successionist" notion of causality: contrary to Hume's view, the same causal stream can produce different outcomes, and different streams can lead to the same outcome. There is ample evidence that many different leadership styles and approaches are associated with similar results. Given this, the search for effective leadership may lead only to contingent conclusions; there likely is no single form of leadership that will be effective in all contexts.

This claim finds support in recent explications of leadership as a social practice situated within particular contexts and helping to constitute those contexts. This notion of social practice has roots in moral, cognitive, and sociocultural theories. Numerous scholars have developed the concept of a social practice (e.g., Bourdieu, 1977; Britzman, 1991; Giddens, 1984; MacIntyre, 1981), and the general idea has been applied to the particularities of educational leadership (e.g., Anderson & Grinberg, 1998; Cherryholms, 1988; Riehl, 1998, 2000).

In brief, a social practice is thought to be a particular way of being in the world, a constellation of understandings, values, and actions that emerges from a particular context (with all of its history, tradition, and physical, ideological, and interactional components) and that helps to either recreate or transform that context. This dialectical and mutually constitutive relationship is integral to the concept of practice. Persons engage in social practices that are well-established and grounded, but they are also agents able to transform both practice and context. They do some things unreflexively, but they can also reflect on their agency and think and act deliberately.

Elaborating this notion with regard to the practice of teaching, Borko (2004) describes a "situative perspective" which views the actions of individuals as individual choices situated within a shared culture of knowledge and practice that is realized at deepening layers of social organization—from the local classroom or school, to the wider district or state policy context, to an even wider community of professionals. Individual action is thus constitutive of the broader context—created by participating in socially organized practices but also serving to co-create and change them. Within such a nested world, phenomena can be studied at any of the various layers, and the unit of analysis can shift accordingly, focusing on individual actors or the entire social system as needed. But the context and activities in which people find themselves are a fundamental aspect of what they themselves do and must be studied. Such a perspective is especially useful because it avoids the temptation to reify either individual characteristics or social group characteristics as fixed and universal. Thus, persons do not do things just because they are African Americans or because they are school principals; they make individual choices within the situated contexts of African American cultural knowledge and practice, or of leadership knowledge and practice. As an example, Riehl (1998) described how an elementary school principal acted during faculty meetings in ways that reflected the widely accepted cultural practice of school leadership situated in elementary schooling and that also served to transform that context and cultural practice, however subtly.

A social practice is moral activity, grounded in values and rules that give the practice coherence and an enduring quality (MacIntyre, 1981). One implication of this is that normative theories as well as empirical evidence can provide warrants for how one might engage in the practice (Riehl, 2000).

Riehl (2000) suggests that a social practice also has an epistemological grounding, since the act of doing something is a way of coming to know about it as well as coming to know oneself and establishing one's identity. Knowledge, identity, and practice are thus intertwined. Gutierrez and Rogoff (2003) echo this, suggesting that identities are not "styles" but instead are a form of social practice: "People live culture in a mutually constitutive manner in which it is not fruitful to tote up their characteristics as if they occur independently of culture, and of culture as if it occurs independently of people" (p. 21). Similarly, Nasir & Saxe (2003) suggest that cultural practices are essential to identity and its enactment.

If school leadership is indeed a social practice, situated within and constitutive of a broader social and cultural context, then studying it would necessitate examining the dynamic nature of this practice and the fluid relationship it has with its context and boundaries. One would need to understand how practitioners themselves make sense of this dynamic relationship. Also, as Borko (2004) suggests, it would be important to understand how the practice is grounded in ever-deepening layers of the social context. This is almost impossible to do in a study that extracts and isolates variables in order to determine causal sequences. It requires a careful and contingent look at circumstances and the enactment of leadership. And it cautions against developing too fixed a notion of school leadership. In this regard, suggestions gleaned from Gutierrez and Rogoff (2003) can help researchers capture the nature of leadership as a social practice. For example, they suggest that certain identity-relevant terms be used as descriptions of regularities (but not determinants) in a cultural pattern rather than as a rigid classification of persons or groups. Reporting research in the past tense would help avoid the connotation that conclusions are intended to be generalized widely over time and space. Background, context factors should be treated as "dynamically changing configurations" that are constitutive of person's agency.

A contingency perspective on organizational effectiveness has long been a prominent feature of organizational theory. Perrow (1986), Woodward (1965) and others provided justification for the adage that there is no one best way to organize, but some ways are more effective than others. Thus, to most scholars of leadership, the notion of a contingent relationship between context and the social practice of leadership will not be surprising, although the constitutive nature of the relationship and its cultural dimensions reflect newer insights.

Making Meaning About the World

A second understanding that colors leadership knowledge development is our understanding of the world and how we come to know it. To many, it is clear that social life has both objective and subjective dimensions. What people experience as "reality" includes material conditions, but also constructions, based on how we respond to our material conditions (and also on the basis of what we don't see or have false consciousness of). These constructions may be in the minds and perceptions of individuals, but they are also "social constructions" based on the co-created and socially shared perceptions of others; we thus know the world both subjectively and intersubjectively (Bernstein, 1976). In the leadership context, this means that leaders participate in the creation and interpretation of their worlds. In the research context, it means that the world being studied has both objective and subjective components, and includes the products of the consciousness of the researcher as well. This observation was introduced to formal social science several decades ago by Berger and Luckmann (1966) and by symbolic interactionists such as Blumer (1969).

This understanding suggests that researchers need to develop appropriate ways to apprehend the subjective and objective features of human life, along with their subjective and objective consequences. This has at least three implications. First, we have to take the "double hermeneutic" seriously and account for it in research designs. By this I refer to Giddens's (1984) assertion that human interpretations run in an iterative cycle. Research begins as an activity of interpreting the human world. But others in the world hear and interpret those first interpretations and adjust their thoughts and actions accordingly, which then changes the world being studied and requires that the initial interpretations be revisited. By way of contrast, biologists studying amoeba can develop any number of interpretations of the amoeba, analyzing why they look and behave as they do. Since amoeba presumably cannot hear or read what the researchers are saying—at least under current biological paradigms—they do not change their character or behavior on the basis of the scientists' interpretations; it is a single hermeneutic.

So, for example, if a leadership researcher interprets and reports her observational data in terms of "distributed leadership," any leader within hearing may in turn interpret the research and adjust their practice toward or away from distributed leadership, thus quickly changing the landscape of leadership practice and requiring a new round of interpretation. This second hermeneutic step, the interpretive work of those being studied, changes the reality into which the researcher is delving, and it must be accounted for. In this way, social science takes on a much more fluid character than the physical sciences typically need to worry about. Researchers must choose research designs that can accommodate the fact that they are shooting at a moving target, so to speak.

Second, the meaning-making processes of the persons who are researchers must be acknowledged. This requires special attention to how to handle thorny issues like disclosing researcher positionalities and accounting for verification and the trustworthiness of findings. Increasingly, researchers are realizing that this is an issue for everyone whose presence in the research process might influence the results.

Third, we also have to think about the meaning-making that the consumers of our research engage in and how they interpret and use information provided through scholarship. This invites us to consider once again which kinds of knowledge count, and why. In the example I described above, the school principal about to assign students to courses may be well-trained to pay special attention to scientific evidence. But what if the evidence is weak or contradictory? What if the fictional account of tracking (in Doyle's novel) sticks in her mind far better than any correlational study? Furthermore, what if our hypothetical principal is not only looking for knowledge to make a definitive decision about tracking, but also wants to provide her teachers with a reading that will sensitize them to the issue, or stir their hearts and minds to try something different, or equip the troops for the long haul of learning to differentiate instruction, or simply encourage the "wide-awakeness" about the world that Maxine Greene (1977) considers so essential to human life? Which kind of knowledge will do the trick?

The Plot-Like Nature of Knowledge

Jerome Bruner (1986) has argued that human beings come to know the world and express what they know in two very broad ways. The first is what he calls the logo-scientific or paradigmatic mode of knowing. In this mode, knowledge is conveyed by categorizing, conceptualizing, and describing phenomena via logical propositions (i.e., declarative sentences) that represent relationships among processes, things, and events. These propositions usually abstract phenomena from the complexity of context and are arrayed in a way that demonstrates some kind of causal ordering of the world. Most of us have been schooled in this mode of knowing and are familiar with its contours. We understand scientific propositions to the degree that we can follow the formal logic behind them and accept their empirical basis in the world of objective, observable reality.

The second method is the narrative mode of knowing, what Bruner (1986) sometimes calls "folk psychology." This, he argues, is the most basic way in which people give meaning to their experiences and organize their knowledge about the world—at least the social world. More prevalent and persuasive than the paradigmatic mode, it is essentially a narrativized epistemology, with knowledge displayed through narratives instead of propositions. These narratives both interpret the world that is experienced and invite further interpretation of the stories themselves. They thus privilege an "agentive Self" (Bruner, 1990, p. 41) who actively experiences and makes sense of the world. Narratives are hermeneutic devices that present fluid, holistic, somewhat imprecisely rendered accounts, in order that the reader or hearer can participate in their interpretation rather than having to accept "the 'sudden death' quality of objectively framed expositions where things are portrayed 'as they are'" (Bruner, 1990, pp. 54–55).

These ideas are important for research on educational leadership, in at least two ways. First, they help to remind us that educational leaders themselves rely on stories—those they tell themselves and those told to them—as well as propositions for making their own meanings about leadership. This is an important insight to keep in mind as we seek to make our scholarship useful to practitioners. Second, they have implications for the ways in which inquiry might be conducted and results might be reported. They challenge oft-held notions of the status hierarchy of knowledge. As Czarniawska (1998) notes, "by the criteria of scientific (paradigmatic) knowledge, the knowledge carried by narratives is not very impressive. Formal logic rarely guides the reasoning, the level of abstraction is low, and the causal links may be established in a wholly arbitrary way" (p. 3). Yet narrative is a main mode of human knowledge and communication. Stories can teach, and be remembered, in ways that propositions cannot. Czarniawska (1997) underscores narrative's ability to maintain an open meaning structure, thus staying true to the "human project" of interpreting the world. Polkinghorne (1988) suggests that readers accept a narrative's conclusion not because of its logical inevitability, but instead because the story coheres through whatever surprises and disclosures it presents. In contrast, scientific knowledge convinces to the degree that it establishes general laws or probable relationships that cover observable events. In the end, it is narrative's fidelity to life as we understand it, its *verisimilitude*, that recommends narrative, as opposed to the so-called *truth* value of logical-scientific knowledge (Bruner, 1986).

Bruner (1986) claims that the paradigmatic and narrative modes of knowing are complementary but not reducible to one another. That is, they reflect two very different ways of creating meaning about the world. In the context of the current debates about "scientific" knowledge, it may seem that only the former mode of knowing would fall under the scientific umbrella. But rather than simply accept the hard boundaries between the two, it might be useful to consider how they are interrelated. For example, Czarniawska (1997) asserts that science itself is built on a narrative of progress that provides its legitimation, whether or not it is acknowledged. In other words, science itself is discursively constituted. Moreover, scientists use narratives in many ways, especially as orienting devices and bumpy vessels of nascent understanding. Scientists tell themselves and each other stories about the world; the stories' gaps and crevices are gradually filled in with the fruits of empirical evidence and logical reasoning as scientific inquiry proceeds.

Beyond that, it seems that scientific propositions and narratives share one particularly important feature: the plot. In the narrative mode, because of its close affinity to literary structure, the concept of plot is invoked regularly. Narrative interpretations of the social world are built around plots as their key organizing features. Events find their meaning in how they relate to the overall plot of the story. "Emplotment" is then the dialectic process of finding the best plot to knit events together into a meaningful whole (Polkinghorne, 1988). For the most part, narrative plots intend to present experience as the result of "the intentionality of human action" (Czarniawska, 1997, p. 18) rather than the rolling out of determinate events that lie almost beyond the control of individuals.

Polkinghorne (1988) claims that this kind of plot, as an end result, is different from the results of scientific reasoning, where relationships among variables are stated in ways that become both explanations of past events and predictions of future events. In contrast, narrative only looks backward to frame an explanation of what has happened, particularly with regard to intentional human action. But this may be overstating the case with regard to social science. Polkinghorne (1988) himself admits that the reasoning behind plot construction and that used for hypothesis generation are similar:

> The recognition or construction of a plot employs the kind of reasoning that Charles Peirce called "abduction," the process of suggesting a hypothesis that can serve to explain some puzzling phenomenon. Abduction produces a conjecture that is tested by fitting it over the "facts." The conjecture may be adjusted to provide a fuller account of the givens . . .
>
> The reasoning used to construct a plot is similar to that used to develop a hypothesis. Both are interactive activities that take place between a concep-

tion that might explain or show a connection among the events and the resistance of the events to fit the construction. (p. 19)

Polkinghorne (1988) goes on to say that:

> The power of explanation by laws comes from its capacity to abstract events from particular contexts and discover ,relationships that hold among all the instances belonging to a category, irrespective of the spatial and temporal context . . . But explanation by means of narrative is contextually related and is therefore different in form from formal science explanation. (p. 21)

While we might concede Polkinghorne this last point in terms of an idealized version of scientific reasoning, the reality typically is much different. Indeed, the original business of science may have been the search for general laws of behavior, encoded as propositions about the relationships among variables, especially causal relationships. And yes, these have frequently been presented as decontextualized, determinate, inviolate relationships, on the surface. But digging deeper, what any scientific model really is, particularly in the social sciences and especially with regard to quantitative analyses, is a probabilistic and conditional chain of events. That is, statistical results generally mean that with a degree of probability—that might be high or low—if one thing happens, this another thing will happen more or less to the strength indicated. Moreover, formal theory building in the social sciences ideally incorporates "scope statements" that specify the conditions under which the observed effects would be expected (Cohen, 1989). (This is also accomplished via control variables.) Scope conditions, variance explained, error terms, confidence intervals, probability levels—all of these regular components of a statistical analysis have the practical function of carrying the contextualization and indeterminacy of the observed events and relationships. If we acknowledge them and take them seriously, it becomes clear that a quantitative analysis has plenty of room for meaningful human action. When joined with the theoretical apparatus that gives the quantitative data its conceptual meaning, the scientific analysis has as much of a plot as a story does.

Bruner and others argue that the narrative plot gives more credence to meaningful human action than to determinate events, that it recognizes the importance of context, and that it is ill-specified enough to permit the reader to do some of the work of interpreting social life. This suggests that narratives are appropriate conveyers of knowledge when there is little trust in, or hope for, any kind of single interpretation for how the world works—a view of the state of the world that, by the way, arguably is held by the authors of the NRC report. Narratives provide credible interpretations and the reader must be an arbiter of their value for explaining the world. But the same could be said of scientific explanations as well. No two readers understand a confidence interval or beta coefficient in exactly the same way; they must apply their own interpretation to the results. My point is not that narrative plots are really more scientific than they appear, but that scientific explanations are more plot-like than they are often acknowledged to be.

Another common distinction between paradigmatic and narrative modes of knowing, instantiated in quantitative and qualitative research, also seems to establish a false dichotomy. It is often stated or implied that quantitative research (propositional knowledge) seeks generalities while qualitative research (narrative knowledge) seeks particularities. But it could be argued that *all* consumers of research, by virtue of their human condition, look for both generalities and particularities. That is, it seems to be the case that humans are inveterate lovers of story who take delight from the recognition of simple, familiar plot lines as well as from the unique twists and turns of particular tales. We want both. Bruner (1990) notes this when he describes narrative's ability to conform to "canonical expectations" and the "deviation or exceptionality" from such expectations (p. 35). Thus, when we read a closely drawn qualitative study, perhaps including admonishments from the author not to overgeneralize, many do just that. We frequently extract generalizations from even the most discrete interpretive research, even when warned against it. (Many a concluding chapter or section of a qualitative research report, however, succumbs to the temptation to overreach toward larger lessons; it is not always the reader's doing alone.) Similarly, we often read statistical research with specific known cases in mind, and accept the quantitative results only if they seem to cover the local stories we know.

The creative tension between patterned regularities and localized variation may be exactly what defines human life, which after all is quite recognizable across time and place. So why not accept the broad plot-like strokes of quantitative research along with the detailed nuances of qualitative studies? Can we not countenance the search for general trends in social reality, embellished by the details of how these general trends work themselves out in particular time-space contexts?

It may be that the problem with quantitative research is not that it generates lawlike statements that subvert or ignore our understandings of local variation, but that its rhetorical structure seems to eliminate any sense of indeterminacy, human intentionality, or meaning-making. Rhetorical tropes such as the pervasive use of the third person omniscient voice, the absence of the first-person subject of the author ("I"), and the use of the continuing present tense may convey too much certainty and objectivity. In addition, variables—the stock and trade of quantitative research—are constructed, measured, and described in ways that eliminate their own tentativeness and variability, their own capacity to represent intentional human action. In his presidential address to the American Sociological Society in 1956, Blumer (1969) identifies this problem:

> We are here faced . . . by the fact that the very features which give variable analysis its high merit—the qualitative constancy of the variables, their clean-cut simplicity, their ease of manipulation as a sort of free counter, their ability to be brought into decisive relation—are the features that lead variable analysis to gloss over the character of the real operating factors in group life, and the real interaction and relations between such factors. (p. 138)

Take the use and measurement of "race" as an example. Uncounted sociologists have treated race as a discrete categorical variable, a convenient distinction that has become a ubiquitous control or explanatory factor in quantitative research. Thanks to qualitative, critical, and interpretive researchers, this approach is hardly tenable anymore, since we now know much more about the fluid, complex, and contested nature of the social construction of race and racial identity for groups and individuals.

Literary theorists and rhetoricians know that we encode and present information and knowledge in a variety of genres, each with their own implicit and explicit rules and conventions (e.g., Fowler, 1989; Swales, 1990; Wellek & Warren, 1963). Human beings learn to read and interpret genres.

Over the past several decades, it has become clear that genres are not merely neutral vessels for carrying information, but they convey information on their own, even to the point of manipulating the receiver (and perhaps the sender as well). In this sense, the rhetoric of quantitative research may create a genre that is constitutive as both a cause and effect of the scientific way of seeing and expressing reality.

Adopting the rhetorics of narrative prose can be a helpful corrective for scientific research. Telling stories, even about quantitative analyses, might disrupt an unwarranted sense of certainty about things. And because narrative is a universal genre, it may make communication more possible between researchers and the wider educational community. As Constas (1998) points out:

> There is little doubt that narrative methodology has spawned a more engaging type of discourse, particularly when one considers the generations of algorithmic writing that were produced in accordance with the style manual of the American Psychological Association . . . Narrative modes of inquiry paired with narrative representation of findings can do much to close the long-standing distance that has existed between the abstract writings of educational researchers and the interests of practicing professionals in the field of education. (p. 30)

Constas cautions, however, that the rhetoric of certainty might be deeply missed by policymakers and others who need parsimonious information that can support "categorical decision-making" for choices regarding whether a program should be funded or not, whether a textbook should be used or not, and so on. To that, we can add a further caveat that it would be highly regrettable if propositions and stories transmuted into one another in ways that obscure the essential elements of science—high quality evidence subjected to careful modes of scrutiny, explained at a level of conceptual abstraction. These are standards to which both propositional and narrative modes of knowledge should be held.

These three observations—about leadership as a social practice, the meaning-making nature of human life, and the importance of plot-like knowledge conveyed in narratives and propositions—suggest that we need more research of more variety, rather than simple "better" research that follows a narrow band of specification. We need more examples of evolving research practices as well as, of course, more evidence about the phenomena they seek to disclose and interpret. And we need to subject this research to continued examination and discussion.

FRAMING FUTURE INQUIRY IN EDUCATIONAL LEADERSHIP

In this concluding section, I offer several suggestions for how research in educational leadership can respond to both the concerns raised by the NRC report on scientific research in education and the additional observations I have made in this essay.

First, echoing the discussion above, research will generate knowledge for the world we live in to the degree that it addresses the full complexity of educational leadership as a meaning-driven, socially situated, interpretive practice. While the search for typical regularities may continue, it should be leavened by an equally vigorous effort to understand the localized nuances that influence leadership. Research in this field should resist the tendency to reify leadership as a technical, rational, and consequential aspect of organizational or system processes. Models of system chaos or complexity (e.g., Cohen, March, & Olsen, 1972; Waldrop, 1992; Wheatley, 1999) and other "messy images" should continue to attract attention as researchers seek to understand how leadership actually works.

A second suggestion is inspired by Borko (2004), who argues for a "situative" approach to research that simultaneously looks at close phenomena and the wider surrounding picture. She suggests that studying social practices at an individual level (e.g., one principal leading one professional development effort in one school) can provide an "existence proof" by generating evidence that a phenomenon does occur. By moving progressively away from the single case, the researcher can keep the individual and the group in focus at the same time by looking at features of the larger system that impact on the individual. To do this kind of research, it is very helpful to have adequate records of practice—artifacts, videotapes, and so on, and to be able to tap directly into people's thinking about their practice—through data collection techniques that allow actors to anticipate, reconstruct, or reflect upon their thinking. These empirical materials provide windows into practice and also generate opportunities for learning for both practitioners and researchers when they are discussed together (Borko, 2004). Borko describes this "multifocal research perspective" in terms of the metaphor of multifocal contact lenses, which are constructed from both near-vision prescriptions and distance-vision prescriptions and work by letting the "visual system" itself learn to select and attend to the appropriate images. In the research context, a multifocal approach permits the gathering and analysis of data that can illuminate the layered complexity of leadership.

Multifocal research clearly has potential for conveying knowledge about the complexities of educational leadership. This leads to a third suggestion, that the field will be strengthened if researchers choose research methods that articulate well with the questions being asked and that can provide persuasive evidence and well-warranted conclusions. The same methods that might be useful in documenting a recurrent causal pattern won't necessarily be appropriate for understanding how actors make sense out of a confounding leadership challenge. Too often, educational leadership researchers have reached for an easy, convenient, or affordable research design rather than doing what is necessary to answer a question fully. An example here is the research on leaders' effects on student achievement. As Hallinger and Heck (1996) have described, much of this research doesn't even include outcome measures that reflect student achievement in any meaningful way. A counterexample would be the research on schools as professional communities, which began quite appropriately with careful case study methodologies to provide initial descriptions and analyses (e.g., Louis, Kruse, & Associates, 1995; Westheimer, 1998) and gradually evolved to include survey methodologies that permitted investigation of broader patterns of action (e.g., Louis, Marks & Kruse, 1996; Marks & Printy, 2003).

Fourth, it is also important for researchers to continue to attend to the tasks of conceptual development, theory building, and theory testing. This claim makes reference to a central tenet about science, which assumes that evidence is indexed to abstract concepts and propositions within a theoretical model or system. As Bernstein (1976) says, "Empirical research without theory is blind, just as theory without empirical research is empty" (p. 14).

The NRC (2002) report addresses this issue in a way that reflects a traditional sequence of generating, testing, and refining theoretical propositions:

> to make progress possible, then, theories, hypotheses, or conjectures must be stated in clear, unambiguous, and empirically testable terms. Evidence

must be linked to them through a clear chain of reasoning . . . there must be a free flow of critical comment. (p. 18)

Interpretive research approaches the task in a different way, with theoretical insights often emerging from data analysis, but it too can benefit from more precision and rigor in the development and use of conceptual insights. And although it is essential to match theory with evidence, the field might additionally benefit from serious efforts to theorize educational leadership along the lines of broad social and cultural analysis. Such efforts could generate provocative new perspectives on, for example, the role of leadership within a culture of individualism, the discursive nature of leadership, or leaders as ethical actors, which then could inform empirical work. In addition, broad theorizing about leadership could include more careful analysis of the meta-narratives that structure our field (Pillow, 2000).

As Thomas (1997) points out, "theories are not simply the playthings of bored academics" (p. 89). At some point, most theories ought to yield insights that can inform practical problems. But practical problem-solving need not drive all theorizing. Ogawa, Goldring, and Conley (2000) claim that the focus of research in educational administration seems to shift quickly because researchers address the "hot topics" that appeal to policy makers, practitioners, and the public press. This, however, may undermine efforts to work continuously and incrementally on a problem or knowledge area. Ogawa and colleagues (2000) suggest that one solution is for the field to consciously organize around problems at the conceptual level. They provide an example, suggesting that research on the organizational dilemma of "hierarchy" could subsume research on various topical issues of interest to practitioners, such as site-based management, teacher leadership, and school choice. This echoes a useful heuristic from Geertz (1973), who introduced the notion of "experience-near and experience-distant concepts" in his approach to anthropology.

Riehl and Firestone (2005) suggest the use of design research methodologies as a way to devote attention both to conceptual and theoretical development of the field and to the creation and refinement of practical interventions. Design research begins with an explicit theory of action that guides the development of practical interventions. Researchers and practitioners work together to implement the interventions and examine the results, moving iteratively between refinement of the theory and improvement of the intervention (Design-Based Research Collective, 2003).

Fifth, as research methods become more rigorous and are paired with solid conceptual tools, it may also be salutary if researchers report more thoroughly the interpretive processes they use in their work. Shaffer and Serlin (2004) claim that "in any kind of inquiry it is a mistake to regard technique as synonymous with interpretation—an unfortunate legacy, perhaps, of sometimes formulaic interpretations of statistical methods" (p. 23). But too often, so-called descriptions of the interpretive process amount to little more than a recitation of canonical techniques—"cross-case analysis," "search for themes," "chi-square testing," and so on.

This applies to quantitative as well as qualitative researchers. We know the familiar script for handling quantitative data in a postpositivist paradigm: formulate a careful hypothesis grounded in a larger theoretical structure, develop a measurement model to test the hypothesis, conduct the observation, conclude whether the hypothesis has been confirmed or not. But this straightforward description omits all of the most interesting interpretive challenges for the researcher. Current debates about the utility of significance tests, effect sizes, and confidence intervals reflect quandaries about the meaning of quantitative results that can boondoggle even the most accomplished statisticians (e.g., Cohen, 1988). As Rosnow and Rosenthal (1989) claim, "surely, God loves the .06 [level of statistical significance] nearly as much as the .05" (as cited in Thompson, 2002, p. 31). These debates hopefully will lead to more meaningful reporting of quantitative results, including discussion of the observed results in light of other studies—what Thompson (2002) terms "meta-analytic thinking" about one's own study.

But it is even more difficult to find good examples or clear advice on the full range of the interpretive task in quantitative research. Consider, for example, this description of the process:

> The scientist experiences vague doubts, emotional disturbance, inchoate ideas. He struggles to formulate the problem, even if inadequately. He studies the literature, scans his own experience and the experience of others. Often he simply has to wait for an inventive leap of the mind. . . . Then the hypothesis is constructed . . . In this process the original problem, and of course the original hypothesis, may be changed . . . Lastly, but not finally, the relation expressed by the hypothesis is tested by observation and experimentation. On the basis of the research evidence, the hypothesis is accepted

or rejected. This information is then fed back to the original problem and it is kept or altered as dictated by the evidence. (Kerlinger, 1964, pp. 16–17)

Kerlinger (1964) calls this "a controlled rational process of reflective inquiry" (p. 17). It is clearly richer and more fraught with risks and potential missteps than is conveyed in the usual quantitative research report, all dressed up in certainty about the hypothesis being tested and the results reported. Interpretive moments occur at different times in the process, especially in comparison to qualitative research. Rather than asking "how can I make sense of these data during and after data collection?" the quantitative researcher engages in theoretical work before and after an explicit test of a hypothesis. Post hoc theorizing sometimes is decried as having no evidentiary value because the propositions are not subjected to an empirical test (Cohen, 1989), but clearly it has a crucial place in the cycle of theory development and testing; one study's post hoc conjectures become another study's testable hypotheses. It would be interesting (and especially helpful to students of the craft) if this interpretive process were more exposed in quantitative research reports.

Although qualitative researchers think and write often about the interpretive challenges they face (e.g., Peshkin, 2000), they too can neglect to describe the twists and turns of their interpretive process, substituting a menu of techniques for the real substance of interpretation. Anfara, Brown, and Mangione (2002) provide a very helpful corrective to this, illustrating several ways in which researchers can report more fully their analytic process. They urge researchers against what they call the "privatization of analysis," in which phrases such as "themes emerged from the data" or "member checks were done" are included almost as "magical incantations." Instead, they argue, researchers must unequivocally present evidence that will answer concerns about the refutability and replicability of the research. For example, they suggest that "documentary tables" can be included to show details of the analysis such as how research questions were indexed to interview protocol questions, how coding proceeded through multiple iterations, and how data were triangulated.

In the realm of interpretation, how much should researchers' own biases and beliefs come into the picture? I suspect that most scholars, qualitative as well as quantitative researchers, have strong value orientations of one type or another regarding their general topics of study. Indeed, it could be argued that if scholars do not have such orientations, they may produce research that is simply not very interesting or relevant. There is a great difference between disinterested research and uninterested research. Consider this statement from a prominent statistician:

> Some activities command more interest, devotion, and enthusiasm from man [sic] than others. So it seems to be with science and art . . . All that seems to be clear is that once men become immersed in scientific research or artistic expression they devote very large portions of their thoughts, energies, and emotions to these activities. . . . Shouldn't we be objective? Shouldn't we develop a hardheaded attitude toward psychological, sociological, and educational phenomena? Yes, of course. But more important is somehow to catch the essential quality of the excitement of discovery that comes from research well done . . . What I am trying to say is that strong subjective involvement is a powerful motivator for acquiring an objective approach to the study of phenomena. It is doubtful that any significant work is ever done without great personal involvement . . . Thus I would encourage students to discuss, argue, debate, and even fight about research. Take a stand. Be opinionated. Later try to soften the opinionation into intelligent conviction and controlled emotional commitment. (Kerlinger, 1964, p. vii)

Since that passage was written, of course, much ink has been spilled over the question of the researcher's connection to her or his work. It is now readily acknowledged that all knowledge is theory-laden and therefore potentially biased; we circle around the fear that researchers may let their prejudices unduly influence their scholarship, but we also seek ways in which researcher positionalities can strengthen the research process. As an example, Tillman (2002) argues that culturally sensitive research—often conducted by persons from social locations similar to those being studied—takes into account deep cultural knowledge and history and enables more accurate interpretations and generalizations. In this vein, Walker (2005) describes how her own positioning as a researcher of color gave her access to data and sensitivity in its interpretation.

The NRC report expresses the hope that the scrutiny of the scientific community will act as a great arbiter and corrective for research quality issues in education. This underscores the sixth suggestion—the need for a lively scholarly discourse in educational leadership. Researchers sometimes forget to position their research explicitly vis-à-vis other research efforts. The result is often a cacophony of voices rather than a swelling chorus leading in fruitful directions. Our field could benefit from the strategic use of research syntheses, meta-analyses, and interpretive reviews of research to help give form and direction to a dispersed enterprise. More intentional specification and use of common concepts, along with operationalization of concepts through easily replicated measurement tools, would also help. Even something as simple as a structured abstract for research articles (Mosteller, Nave, & Miech, 2004) could enhance the prospects of cumulative learning from research. In addition, our research community would be strengthened by examining our own intersubjectivities and biases as a field, and the factors that motivate our work.

Two final suggestions concern how we advance beyond our current research. The world of educational leadership practice is moving very quickly, led by practical reasoning, reflective practice, political ideas, and not just by systematic research. We have to be able to follow current developments and understand them, but also to anticipate what will happen next. Other fields have developed discovery-oriented tools for doing this, and a seventh suggestion is that the educational leadership field considers employing similar tools and strategies. Design research methods offer one kind of window into the future, as do other forms of research-based development. Normative and prescriptive forms of scholarship and even popular accounts of leadership can also provide hints about the future; although they are not forms of science, they can play a role in the scientific enterprise just as luck and accident do.

Finally, in the field of educational leadership, no one seems to have responsibility for "turning insight into impact." The machinery for developing ideas, turning them into tools or products that can be used (even if those products are simply ways of thinking about a problem), marketing and distributing them, and tracking the results hardly exists at all. Burkhardt and Schoenfeld (2003) described how mathematics instructional reform ideas got their walking legs through a rare but happy coincidence of events, resources, and people coming together over a sufficient time frame to make a difference. Rare in any field, this constellation of beneficent forces is something to wish for but not expect. But the present time seems to be as good as any—and better than most—given the amount of attention being directed at educational leadership. It would be a shame to squander this opportunity by haranguing ourselves over whether all of our research is sufficiently scientific; nor should we ignore the very clear mandate to conduct scientific research. We ought to use this time well to focus attention and marshall resources to ensure that *all* of our scholarship really does make a difference.

CONCLUSION

In this chapter, I have argued that the field of educational leadership could benefit by developing many types of useful knowledge, including but not limited to scientific research. Our inquiries could be strengthened by deeper understandings of leadership as a situated social practice and of knowledge development as an interpretive, meaning-making activity that often relies on the use of narrative devices for both discovering and conveying knowledge. These insights could guide leadership research in many productive directions. Ultimately, however, the proof value of what we do lies in the answers we can honestly give to two general questions. First, are we telling a more accurate, more interesting, more informative story of the world that we study; are we getting the central plots and local details right? Does that story lift us up to a higher conceptual level even as it grounds us in the experiences at hand? And second, does our work make a difference? Do our observations and interpretations carry weight and significance; are they convincing to those who see differently than we do? Do they help people do better things?

What the current debates over scientific research suggest is that we will need strength for the long haul. Methodological arguments are turf battles, not only about the methods themselves but also about the knowledge that research generates. As the stakes go up for educational leadership, as people pay more attention to what we know about leadership and as what leaders do becomes linked more closely to particular outcomes for particular students, we can only expect arguments over methodology to become even more heated and perhaps ideological. They will have material outcomes in terms of funding and status and attention, for educational leadership researchers as well as for the leaders themselves. This may be a dilemma to be managed, not a problem to be solved. Perhaps one of the outcomes will be a general rising of the bar; all forms of knowledge development, including so-called scientific research as well as other forms of inquiry, will have to be better in order to have a fair hearing in this complex environment.

Another outcome might be that we develop more tolerance for dialectic. Perhaps the current controversies in educational research are merely a frantic effort to find a "safe harbor" of knowledge that can reliably guide practice. If we can help our field to envision that safe harbor not as a simplistic, unitary body of knowledge, but as a fertile and exciting treasure trove of ideas, we can fit ourselves and others for the new challenges we will most certainly continue to encounter.

Many prominent social theorists, from Giddens to Foucault, have warned about the increasing "administration of human life" as social institutions take control over more domains of human thought and action. On the one hand, scholars in educational leadership generally hope to improve the effectiveness of the social organization and administration of education. On the other hand, we ought to be wary of helping to tighten whatever iron grip on society it holds. We are left, then, with one final question: what kinds of research do we need, and how shall it be conducted, to help restore and retain that which is most humane and social in the human discipline of education?

REFERENCES

Allington, R. (2002). *Big brother and the national reading curriculum: How ideology trumped evidence*. Portsmouth, NH: Heinemann.

Anderson, G. L., & Grinberg, J. (1998). Educational administration as a disciplinary practice: Appropriating Foucault's view of power, discourse, and method. *Educational Administration Quarterly, 34*(3), 329–353.

Anfara,V. A., Jr., Brown, K. M., & Mangione, T. L. (2002). Qualitative analysis on stage: Making the research process more public. *Educational Researcher, 31*(7), 28–38.

Bennis, W. G., & O'Toole, J. (2005). How business schools lost their way. *Harvard Business Review, 83*(5), 96–104.

Berger, P. L., & Luckmann, T. (1966). *The social construction of reality: A treatise in the sociology of knowledge*. Garden City, NY: Doubleday.

Bernstein, R. J. (1976). *The restructuring of social and political theory*. Philadelphia: University of Pennsylvania Press.

Blumer, H. (1969). *Symbolic interactionism: Perspective and method*. Berkeley: University of California Press.

Borko, H. (2004). Professional development and teacher learning: Mapping the terrain. *Educational Researcher, 33*(8), 3–15.

Bourdieu, P. (1977). *Outline of a theory of practice*. New York: Cambridge University Press.

Britzman, Deborah P. (1991). *Practice makes practice: A critical study of learning to teach*. Albany: State University of New York Press.

Bruner, J. S. (1986). *Actual minds, possible worlds*. Cambridge, MA: Harvard University Press.

Bruner, J. (1990). *Acts of meaning*. Cambridge, MA: Harvard University Press.

Burkhardt, H., & Schoenfeld, A. H. (2003). Improving educational research: Toward a more useful, more influential, and better-funded enterprise. *Educational Researcher, 32*(9), 3–14.

Cherryholmes, C. H. (1988). *Power and criticism: Poststructural investigations in education*. New York: Teachers College Press.

Cohen, B. P. (1989). *Developing sociological knowledge: Theory and method*. Chicago: Nelson-Hall.

Cohen, J. (1988). *Statistical power analysis for the behavioral sciences* (2nd ed.). Hillsdale, NJ: Lawrence Erlbaum Associates.

Cohen, M. D., March, J. G., & Olsen, J. P. (1972). A garbage can model of organizational choice. *Administrative Science Quarterly, 17*(1), 1–25.

Collins, P. H. (2000). *Black feminist thought: Knowledge, consciousness, and the politics of empowerment* (2nd ed.). New York: Routledge.

Constas, M. A. (1998). The changing nature of educational research and a critique of postmodernism. *Educational Researcher, 27*(2), 26–33.

Cronbach, J. L. (1975). Beyond the two disciplines of scientific psychology. *American Psychologist, 30*, 671–684.

Czarniawska, B. (1997). *Narrating the organization: Dramas of institutional identity*. Chicago: University of Chicago Press.

Czarniawska, B. (1998). *A narrative approach to organization studies*. Thousand Oaks, CA: Sage Publications.

Design-Based Research Collective. (2003). Design-based research: An emerging paradigm for educational inquiry. *Educational Researcher, 32*(1), 5–8.

Doyle, R. (1996). *The woman who walked into doors*. New York: Penguin Books.

Drazen, J. M. (2003). Controlling research trials. *New England Journal of Medicine, 348*(14), 1377–1380.

Eisenhart, M. (2005). Science plus: A response to the responses to *Scientific Research in Education. Teachers College Record, 107*(1), 52–58.

Eisenhart, M., & Towne, L. (2003). Contestation and change in national policy on "scientifically based" education research. Educational Researcher, 32(7), 31–38.

Erickson, F. (2005). Arts, humanities, and sciences in educational research and social engineering in federal education policy. Teachers College Record, 107(1), 4–9.

Erickson, F., & Gutierrez, K. (2002). Culture, rigor, and science in educational research. Educational Researcher, 31(8), 21–24.

Feuer, M. J., Towne, L., & Shavelson, R. J. (2002). Scientific culture and educational research. Educational Researcher, 31(8), 4–14.

Finn, C. E., Jr. (1988). What ails education research. Educational Researcher, 17(1), 5–8.

Fowler, A. (1989). Kinds of literature. Oxford, UK: Oxford University Press.

Gee, J. P. (2005). It's theories all the way down: A response to Scientific Research in Education. Teachers College Record, 107(1), 10–18.

Geertz, C. (1973). Interpretation of cultures: Selected essays. New York: Basic Books.

Giddens, A. (1984). The constitution of society. Berkeley: University of California Press.

Greene, M. (1977). Toward wide-awakeness: An argument for the arts and humanities in education. Teachers College Record, 79(1), 119–125.

Gutierrez, K. D., & Rogoff, B. (2003). Cultural ways of learning: Individual traits or repertoires of practice. Educational Researcher, 32(5), 19–25.

Hallinger, P., & Heck, R. L. (1996). Reassessing the principal's role in school effectiveness: A review of the empirical research: 1980–95. Educational Administration Quarterly, 32(1), 5–44.

Kerlinger, F. N. (1964). Foundations of behavioral research: Educational and psychological inquiry. New York: Holt, Rinehart and Winston.

Kuhn, T. S. (1970). The structure of scientific revolutions. Chicago: University of Chicago Press.

Lather, P. (1991). Getting smart: Feminist research and pedagogy with/in the postmodern. New York: Routledge.

Louis, K. S., Kruse, S., & Associates. (1995). Professionalism and community: Perspectives on reforming urban schools. Thousand Oaks, CA: Corwin Press.

Louis, K. S., Marks, H. M., & Kruse, S. (1996). Teachers' professional community in restructuring schools. American Educational Research Journal, 33(4), 757–798.

MacIntyre, A. (1981). After virtue. London: Duckworth.

Marks, H. M., & Printy, S. M. (2003). Principal leadership and school performance: An integration of transformational and instructional leadership. *Educational Administration Quarterly, 39*(3), 370–397.

Maxwell, J. A. (2004). Causal explanation, qualitative research, and scientific inquiry in education. *Educational Researcher, 33*(2), 3–11.

Mayer, R. E. (2000). What is the place of science in educational research? *Educational Researcher*, issue no. 38–39.

Moss, P. (2005). Toward "epistemic reflexivity" in educational research: A response
to *Scientific Research in Education. Teachers College Record, 107*(1), 19–29.

Mosteller, F., Nave, B., & Miech, E. J. (2004). Why we need a structured abstract
in education research. *Educational Researcher, 33*(1), 29–34.

Nasir, N. I. S., & Saxe, G. B. (2003). Ethnic and academic identities: A cultural
practice perspective on emerging tensions and their management in the lives of
minority students. *Educational Researcher, 32*(5), 14–18.

National Institute of Child Health and Development. (2000). Report of the National
Reading Panel. Teaching children to read: An evidence-based assessment of the
scientific research literature on reading and its implications for reading instruction. Retrieved November 10, 2004, from http://www.nichd.nih.gov/publications/
nrp/smallbook.htm.

National Research Council (NRC) Committee on Scientific Principles for Education Research. (2002). *Scientific research in education*. R. J. Shavelson, &
L. Towne (Eds.). Washington, DC: National Academy Press.

Ogawa, R. T., Goldring, E. B., & Conley, S. (2000). Organizing the field to improve research on educational administration. *Educational Administration
Quarterly, 36*(3), 340–357.

Perrow, C. (1986). *Complex organizations: A critical essay* (3rd ed.). New York:
Random House.

Peshkin, A. (2000). The nature of interpretation in qualitative research. *Educational Researcher, 29*(9), 5–9.

Pillow, W. S. (2000). Deciphering attempts to decipher postmodern educational
research. *Educational Researcher, 29*(5), 21–24.

Polkinghorne, D. E. (1988). *Narrative knowing and the human sciences*. Albany:
State University of New York Press.

Riehl, C. (1998). We gather together: Work, discourse, and constitutive social action in elementary school faculty meetings. *Educational Administration Quarterly, 34*(1), 91–125.

Riehl, C. (2000). The principal's role in creating inclusive schools for diverse students: A review of normative, empirical, and critical literature on the practice of
educational administration. *Review of Educational Research, 70*(1), 55–81.

Riehl, C., & Firestone, W. A. (2005). What research methods should be used to study educational leadership? In W. A. Firestone & C. Riehl (Eds.), *A new agenda for research in educational leadership* (pp. 156–170). New York: Teachers College Press.

Rosnow, R. L., & Rosenthal, R. (1989). Statistical procedures and the justification of knowledge in psychological science. *American Psychologist, 44,* 1276–1284.

Schoenfeld, P., & Scheiman, J. (2003). An evidence-based approach to studies of gastrointestinal therapies. *Clinical Gastroenterology and Hepatology, 1*(1), 57–63.

Shaffer, D. W., & Serlin, R. C. (2004). What good are statistics that don't generalize? *Educational Researcher, 33*(9), 14–25.

Shavelson, R. J. (2002). Lee J. Cronbach, 1916–2001. *Educational Researcher, 31*(2), 37–39.

Stokes, D. E. (1997). *Pasteur's quadrant: Basic science and technical innovation.* Washington, DC: Brookings Institution Press.

Swales, J. M. (1990). *Genre analysis.* Cambridge: Cambridge University Press.

Thomas, G. (1997). What's the use of theory? *Harvard Educational Review, 67*(1), 75–104.

Thompson, B. (2002). What future quantitative social science research could look like: Confidence intervals for effect sizes. *Educational Researcher, 31*(3), 25–32.

Tillman, L. (2002). Culturally sensitive research approaches: An African-American perspective. *Educational Researcher, 31*(9), 3–12.

U.S. Congress. (2001). *No Child Left Behind Act of 2001.* Washington, DC: Author.

von Bertalanffy, L. (1968). *General system theory: Foundations, development, applications.* New York: G. Braziller.

Waldrop, M. M. (1992). *Complexity: The emerging science at the edge of order and chaos.* New York: Simon & Schuster.

Walker, V. S. (2005). After methods, then what? A researcher's response to the report of the National Research Council. *Teachers College Record, 107*(1), 30–37.

Wellek, R., & Warren, A. (1963). *Theory of literature.* Harmondsworth: Penguin Books.

Westheimer, J. (1998). *Among school teachers: Community, autonomy, and ideology in teachers' work.* New York: Teachers College Press.

What Works Clearinghouse. (2004). *WWC evidence standards.* Retrieved May 27, 2005, from http://www.whatworks.ed.gov/reviewprocess/standards.html.

Wheatley, M. J. (1999). *Leadership and the new science: Discovering order in a chaotic world* (2nd ed.). San Francisco, CA: Berrett-Koehler Publishers.

Woodward, J. (1965). *Industrial organization: Theory and practice*. London: Oxford University Press.

Yatvin, J., Weaver, C., & Garan, E. (2003). Reading first: Cautions and recommendations. *Language Arts, 81*(1), 28–33.

Index

About the Editors and Contributors

Fenwick W. English is the R. Wendell Eaves Distinguished Professor of Educational Leadership in the School of Education at the University of North Carolina at Chapel Hill. He is the editor of the Sage *Handbook of Educational Leadership* (2006) and the Sage *Encyclopedia of Educational Leadership and School Administration* (2006). He also authored *The Postmodern Challenge to the Theory and Practice of Educational Administration* in 2003. He is a former middle school principal in California and superintendent of schools in New York. In higher education he has served as a department chair, dean, and vice-chancellor of academic affairs. Currently he is a member of the University Council for Educational Administration (UCEA) Executive Committee and president elect of UCEA. His research interest centers on the epistemology of professional practice.

Gail C. Furman is a Professor of Educational Leadership and Program Coordinator at Washington State University and served as President of UCEA in 2000–2001. In addition to her recent work on research perspectives in the field, her research interests include moral leadership, an ecological perspective on social justice, and the concept of community in schools. Recent publications include the book *School as Community: From Promise to Practice*; a chapter on "Leadership for Democratic Community in Schools" (with Robert J. Starratt) in the NSSE yearbook; and articles in the *Journal of Educational Administration* and *Educational Administration Quarterly* (*EAQ*). Her articles in *EAQ* have been recognized with the Davis Award for outstanding article in 2004 (Honorable Mention) and 1998.

Carol F. Karpinski is an Assistant Professor at the Peter Sammartino School of Education at Fairleigh Dickinson University and the Director of the Master of Arts in teaching program. She has held teaching and administrative positions at the middle and secondary school levels. Her research deals with teacher unions, social justice, and education activists during the African American civil rights movement. She has presented numerous papers at American Educational Research Association (AERA), UCEA, and the History of Education Society meetings. Her publications include forthcoming articles in *Urban Education* and the *Journal of Educational Administration*.

Catherine A. Lugg is an Associate Professor of Education, in the department of Educational Theory, Policy and Administration, at the Graduate School of Education, Rutgers University, and the Associate Director for Publications for the University Council for Educational Administration (UCEA). She is also a Senior Associate Editor for the *Journal of Gay and Lesbian Issues in Education*. Her research interests include educational politics and policy, social and political history, and queer theory. She has published in *Educational Administration Quarterly*, *Educational Policy*, *Education and Urban Society*, *Journal of School Leadership*, *Pennsylvania History*, and *The American Journal of Semiotics*. Her books include *For God & Country: Conservatism and American School Policy*, and *Kitsch: From Education to Public Policy*.

Margaret Terry Orr is on the faculty of Bank Street College, where she directs the Future School Leaders Academy, a university-district partnership program with seventeen suburban school districts. She chairs the Teaching in Educational Administration-SIG of AERA and co-chairs the UCEA/TEA-SIG Taskforce on Evaluating Leadership Preparation Programs, and is a senior consultant on the Stanford University study of exemplary leadership preparation and support programs, funded by the Wallace Foundation. Much of her research publications and presentations address the conceptual and methodological issues in evaluating leadership preparation.

Carolyn Riehl is an Associate Professor and Program Coordinator of the Educational Leadership Program at Columbia University. She has spent the 2005–2006 academic year as the Julius and Rosa Sachs Distinguished Lecturer at Teachers College, Columbia University. She co-chaired a recent task force on research for AERA's Division A (also sponsored by UCEA) and is the co-editor of a volume based on this work, *A New Agenda for Research in Educational Leadership* (2005). Her research interests include leadership for equity and excellence in diverse school contexts, organizational theory as it informs school improvement, and public engagement in education.

Carolyn M. Shields is a Professor of Educational Leadership and Chair of the Department of Educational & Leadership at the University of Illinois at Urbana-Champaign. She is past President of the Canadian Association for Studies in Educational Administration, a board member of the Commonwealth Council for Educational Administration and Leadership, and a member of several ministry advisory committees. Her research and teaching interests relate to leadership for social justice and academic excellence in diverse settings nationally and internationally.

Linda C. Tillman is an Associate Professor in the Educational Leadership Program at the University of North Carolina at Chapel Hill. Her research interests include leadership theory, the education of *all* children, particularly African Americans in K–12 and post secondary education; mentoring African American teachers, administrators, and faculty; and, the use of racially and culturally sensitive qualitative research approaches. She serves on the American Educational Research Association (AERA) Annual Meeting Policies and Procedures Committee and is Chairperson of the AERA Division A (Administration) Mentoring Committee. Recent publications include "Culturally Sensitive Research Approaches: An African American Perspective" in *Educational Researcher*, "African American Principals and the Legacy of *Brown*" in the *Review of Research in Education*. She is also the guest editor of special issues of *The International Journal of Qualitative Studies in Education*, titled "Research on the Color Line: Perspectives on Race, Culture and Qualitative Research" and *Educational Administration Quarterly*, titled "Pushing Back Resistance: African American Discourses on School Leadership." Tillman is the 2004 recipient of the Early Career Contribution Award from the American Educational Research Association Committee on Scholars of Color in Education.

Michelle D. Young is the Executive Director of the University Council for Educational Administration and a faculty member in Educational Leadership and Policy Analysis at the University of Missouri, Columbia. Young's scholarship focuses on how school leaders and school policies can ensure equitable and quality experiences for all students and adults who learn and work in schools. She is the recipient of the William J. Davis award for the most outstanding article published in a volume of the *Educational Administration Quarterly*. Her work has also been published in the *Review of Educational Research*, the *Educational Researcher*, the *American Educational Research Journal*, the *Journal of School Leadership*, the *International Journal of Qualitative Studies in Education*, and *Leadership and Policy in Schools*, among other publications.